Anson's Glory: Ansonia and Phelps-Dodge

A Pictorial History

Elizabeth Crossland Matricaria

Order this book online at www.trafford.com
or email orders@trafford.com

Most Trafford titles are also available at major online book retailers.

Printed in the United States of America.

ISBN: 978-1-4251-2953-8 (sc)
ISBN: 978-1-4669-8973-3 (hc)
ISBN: 978-1-4251-3090-9 (e)

Trafford rev. 04/15/2013

 www.trafford.com

North America & international
toll-free: 1 888 232 4444 (USA & Canada)
phone: 250 383 6864 ✦ fax: 812 355 4082

To
my inspiring and devoted daughter
Sharon Louise
with love

CONTENTS

PART I

"THE PRINCELY MERCHANT"

PART II

ANSONIA

PART III

ANSON G. PHELPS LEGACY AND PROGENY

PART IV

ANSON G. PHELPS BUSINESS LEGACIES

PART V

SEEDS OF HOPE

PART VI

PROLOGUE

I owe this writing to an awareness of the changes in my hometown of Ansonia, Connecticut, since it was founded as a manufacturing village in 1844. I wondered what its founder, Anson Greene Phelps, of whom I knew little, would now plan for his village as it joins other faded manufacturing cities of America. Anson's name is on the city's official seal and on the memorial plaque of the Ansonia public library, yet popular knowledge of the actual man has practically disappeared. His city of glory now seems to be in camouflage.

In 2001, when I moved from Ansonia in the Lower Naugatuck River Valley to Avon in the Farmington River Valley, I discovered I was close to Simsbury, Anson's birthplace. There, the family name of Phelps is memorialized, yet popular knowledge of Anson's connection to Ansonia seems vague, lost, or inconsequential.

My interest was piqued and grew into a research project to find the spirit and vision behind this founder's lifework. I watched the niche in history belonging to Anson Green Phelps and his legacies come alive.

Through the prism of the twenty-first century, *Anson's Glory: Ansonia and Phelps-Dodge* focuses on mankind at the beginning of America's Industrial Era.

Elizabeth Crossland Matricaria
Avon, Connecticut, USA
March 2013

PART I

"THE PRINCELY MERCHANT"

Chapter One

ANSON

His world did not seem fair. He was crying again. His father, Lieutenant Thomas Phelps, finally came home from the war, but then he died. The family of five did not have enough food, and then his mother died.

He was *so very* hungry. *What could* he do? *What would* he do?

*

The boy did not know his family lineage, nor did he understand the circumstances that brought him to the point of crying for food in despair.

He could not imagine that, by virtue of his talents and ceaseless endeavors, as well as by his future adult demeanor and dealings, he would one day be heralded in the business centers of America and Europe as New York City's "Princely Merchant." He could never imagine that such a title would be only the beginning of his achievements.

The boy, Anson Greene Phelps, was an eighteenth century descendant of English immigrants, and a sixth generation American. His lineage was linked to the twelfth and thirteenth century family of Henry Guelph, the Duke of Bavaria, and his famous nephew,

Frederick, who was the celebrated medieval leader known in Germany as the "Lord of Peace." Frederick was also known as the "King of Lombardy," with many followers in Florence. The Guelphs (Phelps in English) led the warriors, who were also called the Welfs, into fierce battles supporting Christianity against tyranny.

Anson's more immediate ancestors were among the many Puritans who fled persecution during the 1625-1649 reign of King Charles II. They were the first of the Phelps Family to leave England for America. "Gentleman" William Phelps as head of the family, his wife, and his brothers, George and Richard, with children, arrived near Boston Harbor on the ship *Mary and John* in 1630.

The ship's Captain Squeb proved to be an excellent seaman, competent under the vagaries of ocean sailing. He was also a prudent man, and refused to sail into the treacherous Charles River without a pilot boat or navigation chart.

His ship carried 140 religious passengers who, after the arduous three-month voyage, anticipated landing in Boston. When they were put ashore on the section of land south of Boston named Nantaskett, they did not hesitate to amply express, in questionable vernacular, the displeasure they felt.

Eventually, part of their extended Phelps family ventured southwest into the Connecticut River Valley and settled in Windsor for more than three generations. In that third generation, a grandson of George Phelps, named Thomas, was born. He later married Hannah Phelps, a granddaughter of "Gentleman William," fortifying the Phelps genes.

In 1741, Thomas and Hannah had a son also named Thomas. In manhood, young Thomas married Dorothy Lamb Woodbridge and they moved from Windsor to Simsbury, a place named in memory of the Symondsbury parish in Dorset, England, home to many of its settlers. Thomas purchased 185 acres of Simsbury land for his wife and family. At the age of twenty-five, he owned a half-interest in the saw and gristmill on Hop Brook in Simsbury.

Dorothy's ancestors had also arrived on the 1630 voyage of the *Mary and John*. Her grandfather, Timothy Woodbridge, was the pastor of the local Congregational Church. When Thomas, Dorothy's husband of ten years, was thirty-two he was caught in the fervor of the Revolutionary War, and patriotically volunteered to serve in the Colonial Army. He left his family and mill to enlist with his fellow villagers.

Two years later, Thomas received his commission as second lieutenant in the Regiment of Artificers (specialized mechanics). He served under the leadership of Generals Greene, Washington, Putnam, and Heath.

He developed a special respect for General Nathaniel Greene, Washington's trusted deputy. His regard for him was such that when his fourth son was born in 1781, he gave him Greene as his middle name. In honor of English Admiral George Anson, who circumnavigated the globe from 1744 through 1749, he had given this son, Anson, as his first name.

Anson was six years old when Lieutenant Thomas Phelps returned from the war in 1787. The Continental Currency had been devalued and the Colonies were in financial distress. His family was caught in a downward spiral of poverty. Living conditions deteriorated, and sickness and hardships overwhelmed them.

Thomas gained construction work rebuilding the blockhouse of the Newgate Prison; but, fell ill and was unable to continue working. In bankruptcy, he died of pneumonia at the age of forty-eight.

Dorothy, his forty-four year old widow, married

Isaac Case of the Bushy Hill section of Simsbury. Conditions continued to be desperate, and in 1792, she also died. George Augustus, one of her sons, had died in 1778, but William, Thomas, and ten-year old Anson were left as orphans.

Anson had been a student at the Congregational Church School. After his mother died, the minister rescued him and became his legal guardian, and he resumed attendance at the school. When Anson turned fourteen, as was the custom for boys at that time, he followed the apprenticeship path and prepared to earn a living.

He carried his worldly possessions in a bag, and walked the dirt roads from his sanctuary in Simsbury to the Connecticut State Capital of Hartford. There Anson began learning the trade of leather tanning and saddlery.

His years of deprivation continued to affect his health, and it became impossible for him to finish his term, confined in the atmosphere of leather tanning. In an attempt to gain strength, Anson left his assignment and found a fresh air outdoor job, working on a farm in West Simsbury.

One fateful day, he saw notices of a scheduled religious revival meeting. Attracted by memories of his earlier rescue by his minister, he decided to attend. The service was so moving that he joined others in making his whole-hearted public confession of faith. It proved to be a defining moment in his life.

At the age of eighteen, Anson, with his older brother Thomas, applied to Reverend Jeremiah Hallock for membership in the Congregational Church at South Canton. There, in May 1799, they made the binding Congregationalist "Covenant with the Lord" and were dedicated to "walk with their fellowman, in all of God's ways."

A short time later, Anson's two brothers and his cousin Job Phelps decided to "Go West." By then, Anson was more healthy and mature and chose to finish his apprenticeship in Hartford. He not only finished the program, he added the study of Mercantile Operations.

Almost immediately he began his own business of making and selling saddles, trunks, and other leather goods. He opened a store and added tinware to his leather goods, then peddled his products from door to door. He traveled to New York City and increased his trade offerings. Soon a notice appeared in the *Hartford Courant* that indicated his expansion:

> Anson G. Phelps has just returned from New York, a General assortment of Groceries, Crockery, and Stoneware. In the store lately occupied by Talcott and Day, 15 rods north of the church, which he will sell on liberal terms N.B. Fresh flour

Anson began to realize that he was innately shrewd and adept at mercantile operations and gained confidence in himself. It was the era of increased travel by pioneers; and saddles, satchels, trunks, and other leather goods were in demand. His business flourished.

He began to widen his search for opportunities beyond the New England states, and found a great need for his wares in South Carolina. While there, he observed the great abundance of cotton and envisioned the potential of its future. Anson calculated that if he added cotton to his trade, it might even exceed the profitability of his leather business.

Upon returning to Hartford, he erected a brick building, named the "Phelps Block" on North Main Street to accommodate his cotton trade shipments.

He then expanded his import and export mercantile operations with a sloop called, *Mary Ann.* She was the first of what was to be his fleet of ocean-going vessels.

Another advertisement appeared in a September 1803 issue of the *Courant.* It was embellished with a small woodcut of a sailing ship:

For Charleston (SC)
The Sloop Mary Ann
R. Chase, Master
Will sail the 1st of October
For Freight or Passage
To ANSON G. PHELPS

On voyages to South Carolina to purchase cotton, Anson had cobblestones from Connecticut loaded on the ship as ballast. Upon arrival they were sold to pave the streets of Charleston.

Anson faithfully kept a diary and one night in March 1806, he wrote "my conscience is free of offense and my finances allow it," and that he felt "in a position to marry."

The following October, he married Olivia Egleston. She was born in Middletown, Connecticut and was three years younger than Anson. Her English ancestors had also arrived in America on the *Mary and John.*

Anson, who frequently praised and gave thanks to his Heavenly Father in his diary, upon the occasion of his marriage, entered "He has been pleased to join my hand with one of the best women."

Olivia and Anson spent their next nine years in Hartford, during which time Elizabeth, Melissa, Caroline Olivia (who did not survive), and Caroline, the first four of their eight children, were born.

As husband and father, Anson wasted no time. He provided for his family, and continued to tend to his store and trading business; all while searching for opportunities to expand his mercantile operations.

(The Phelps Family of America)

Coincidental to this timing, Great Britain was spreading her commerce worldwide. Anson promptly began trading American cotton for the products of the English mills in Liverpool, Manchester, Birmingham, and other industrial centers.

Chapter Two

FATEFUL CIRCUMSTANCES

Anson Greene Phelps was a pious man and during his years in Hartford, he and his family devotedly attended church and prayer meetings. It was there that they became acquainted with David Lowe Dodge and his wife Sarah. They were new in the area and had recently moved from Norwich to Hartford with their young children. The families had much in common and a great friendship developed.

Both men were merchants and deeply religious; and, both traveled to New York City to improve their business interests. Their common goal was to conduct business in accordance with their religious beliefs. They habitually analyzed and evaluated their actions, and concentrated on eliminating any possible evil in their work, as well as in their private lives. Most of all, they held to their vows to help with God's work and to spread His Word. Great lamentations ensued over any possible inequities.

There was however, one distinct difference between the two men. Anson had been primed to fight poverty, and was driven by memories of his childhood trauma of poverty, hunger, grief, and sickness. A deep and lasting impression was made when his church minister rescued him. His sense of helplessness was relieved when he learned to trust his Creator and evaluate the lessons for living found in The Bible.

Faith became an integral part of Anson's life. It was reinforced when he felt the power of his given talents. Grateful, he unfailingly renewed his "Covenant with God" and vowed to walk with his fellowman. He made relevant notations in his diary throughout his life.

His chosen lifestyle kept him very busy. In time he realized he had become a slave to his work ethic. It was reflected in his writings and mingled with yearnings for more personal pleasures. Yet, there is no indication that Anson made any effort to free himself from the sublime motivation of using his God-given talents to fight poverty, secure his family's welfare, and help to improve the lot of his fellowman.

✱

Anson's expanding trade business led him to move the main location of his operations from Hartford to New York in 1812. He also needed a partner, and chose Elisha Peck, a friend who had moved from Berlin, Connecticut to New York. They established the metal and cotton-trading firm of the Phelps-Peck Company, and became merchant shippers.

The War of 1812 with Great Britain began almost immediately after the firm was established. The Royal Navy disrupted trade, and blockades not only prevented the Phelps-Peck overseas import and export business, but also threatened its coastal trade routes.

A story was told that on a day when Anson was aboard his ship, carrying lumber from Hartford to Block

Island, a Royal Navy ship was spotted. The master of the Phelps sloop was so intimidated, he prepared to turn back to Hartford. In annoyance, Anson took his place at the helm, and sailing close to shore, delivered his cargo to Block Island without incident.

When the war ended in 1814, with the signing of the *Treaty of Ghent*, Anson moved his family from Hartford to 83 Beekman Street in New York City. He quickly became part of the new "Down-East" Puritan settlers, who joined the earlier established English, Dutch, and German businessmen. He added his unique business style to the development of commerce along the waterfront at Burling Slip. In 1815, he expanded his trade in metals and this ad appeared:

The subscriber wishes to announce that he will open his Commission Warehouse on or about June 1, 1815, at the stand No. 29 Burling Slip. His principal line will be the Metal Commission and he will offer stock received by recent arrivals consisting of: 62 Boxes Tin-plates; 200 lbs. India Block Tin; 1200 lbs. Old Copper; 899 Iron Wire for sale on liberal terms.

Anson G. Phelps   29 Burling Slip

PS All orders will receive expeditious attention, and Mr. Phelps hopes for a liberal share of your patronage.

*

One of the consequences of the War of 1812 was that America learned to be self-sufficient. As large groups of people migrated west, new industries increased the demand for metals. Anson formed another partnership with Elisha Peck and sent him to England to manage an additional division of their metal and cotton trade. American cotton was sent there for the mills of Lancashire, England, and English metals and products were sent to the six-story Phelps-Peck and Company warehouse at the corner of Cliff and Fulton streets in New York City.

*

As America grew between 1812 and 1828, Anson continued to expand his business. The seven new states of Louisiana, Indiana, Mississippi, Illinois, Alabama, Maine, and Missouri were admitted to the Union. Not only did the United States of America become a country of twenty-four states; it became a country with three great water highways, the Mississippi, Ohio, and Missouri rivers, arteries for trade and transportation. Anson did not miss the opportunity of expanding his business by way of the mighty rivers.

Phelps-Peck had already developed a large coastal trade business using the "Phelps Shipping Agency" fleet of sailing schooners, and were able to send New England peddlers up the great rivers to travel inland and deliver their import-export wares to the settlements.

The peddlers were colorful and friendly characters, who followed the tradition set in the earliest Colonial times. They carried products on their backs, on packhorses, or in wagons, and went deep into the far-flung pioneering areas.

The coastal regions of New England and the Middle

Atlantic States relied upon ocean-going ships to service their markets. Using his pre-emptive commercial vision, Anson created a scheduled packet-boat service called "The Charleston Ship Lane" and joined his shipping business with those of other merchants to connect New York City with South Carolina.

✻

The growth of self-sufficiency in the states fostered the spread of industries and augmented America's involvement in the Industrial Era. Investors from foreign countries became interested in the New World and the number of immigrants to the Atlantic seaboard increased.

Chapter Three

THE NEW YORKER

By 1817, Phelps-Peck was well established in New York as a metal trading company and Anson began investing in many new American projects. In New Jersey, he bought the Dover Bank, an iron foundry, and an iron mine. In New York City, he invested in real estate, banking and insurance.

By 1825, forty-four year old Anson Greene Phelps had become a world-renowned trader and an esteemed New Yorker with friends and acquaintances worldwide. His mild and amiable personality combined with strict integrity, tenacity of purpose, and a high level of energy inspired young men. He was considered a model for success.

Anson did not neglect to continue following the tenets of his religion and attended weekly prayer meetings in New York. By 1825 his observance of the Sabbath had evolved into an active role.

On Sunday evenings, the streets of New York remained deserted in observance of the Sabbath.

Yet, young men in formal attire were out walking and converging at the Anson Greene Phelps residence.

Anson, host of the New York Men's Bible Society weekly prayer meetings, opened his door to admit guests. His keen appraising glance greeted each arrival with a personal welcome. Anson's dark hair had a slight tinge of gray. His dark eyes, bright with interest, overshadowed his aquiline nose, firmly held full lips, and angular chin.

The doors of his home were opened to extend his parlors, and additional seating was improvised to accommodate the crowd. Member guests crowded together as they paid close attention to the preaching of the Princeton Theological Seminary students.

However, at each meeting the intent gathering was likely aware of the three attractive Phelps daughters. Anson's dynasty promise, Elizabeth, Melissa, and Caroline always attended and sat in the back.

*

In 1828, disaster struck the Phelps-Peck Metal Trade Business. Its six-story Cliff Street warehouse, built of wood and subject to heavy stresses, collapsed. Anson's only son, Anson Jr., just missed being present. However, personal tragedy did not escape the family. Anson's confidential assistant, Josiah Stokes, the betrothed of his daughter, Caroline, died in the collapse.

It was a time of mourning and financial upheaval. Entries in Anson's diary that year reveal his distress from feelings of responsibility and loss. Personal recovery time was needed and Anson, with his wife Olivia and daughter Caroline, voyaged to Liverpool, England to visit the oldest daughter, Elizabeth, wife of Daniel James. Anson had channeled his remorse and fear of poverty into a devoutly renewed "Covenant with God." He vowed to dedicate himself more intently to philanthropy if he managed to recover his business losses. He began calculated action. His plan would involve finding a new partner.

Anson's family kinship with the family of David and Sarah Dodge had grown through the years since their meetings in Hartford. Their son William grew to be a very promising young man and Anson's daughter, Melissa, fell in love with him. Anson was pleased to give his blessing to their marriage. He decided he needed to search no further than William for a partner in his new plan.

(Phelps-Dodge Company)
William Earle Dodge

First he bought out the Elisha Peck partnership, except for the wire mill at Haverstraw on the Hudson River, their first successful venture. Then, Anson offered his new son-in-law, William Earle Dodge who was an experienced merchant, a junior partnership in the re-organization of his business.

Under the name of Phelps-Dodge Company, Anson continued with his import and export trade. In 1834, the company headquarters opened at the address of the former Phelps-Peck warehouse on Cliff Street.

To handle his growing business in England, Anson organized a new branch. He thought it fitting to offer Daniel James, also a merchant and the husband of his eldest daughter Elizabeth, a partnership in what would be called the Phelps-James Company.

The changes effectively split his import-export business into two countries under two separate names, Phelps-Dodge Company in New York City, USA and Phelps-James Company in Liverpool, England. Anson then proceeded to divide his financial interests. He retained two-thirds and allocated a sixth to each of sons-in-law, William Dodge and Daniel James.

Soon, the Phelps-Dodge partners were known as New York's highly esteemed merchants. They and their families were active members of Reverend Gardiner Spring's Presbyterian Church on Beekman Street. While savoring business success, the partners expressed their natural joy by performing deeds of benevolence for their fellow men.

Anson actively supported the American Bible Society, the American Board of Commissioners for Foreign Missions, the American Missionary Society, the Colonization Society, and the Blind Asylum of New York City. At one time or another, he served as president of all of those organizations. The "House of the Phelps-Dodge Company" became known as "The Christian Merchants of New York."

Anson was financially able to continue making additions to his trade business with ventures similar to those he had begun in 1817. Well aware of what promised to be valuable in times of changing markets, he followed what his vision and pre-emptive style of business dictated, to enhance the balance and value of his company.

Earlier, William Earle Dodge had acquired a thousand-acre tract of timberland from a debtor in Tioga County, Pennsylvania. The holding sparked Anson's pre-emptive business sense in 1833, when Hezekial Stowell put the under-funded Manchester mills and 25,000 acres of timberland near William's tract on the market. Anson and William added it as a new Phelps-Dodge holding.

The Manchester method of sending manufactured lumber down Pine creek was deemed to be dangerous and its success uncertain. Instead, under Phelps-Dodge ownership, the logs were floated down stream, secured in a boom or harbor, and lumber was manufactured near the river. The Manchester mills were abandoned and new mills were built on Pine creek near a railroad junction. Buildings and sawmills were constructed at various points along the forestland of creeks and rivers. Then, the thirteen to fifteen feet sections of oak, white pine, and hemlock went to Chesapeake Bay by way of the Susquehanna River to Port Deposit.

Upon an 1836 occasion of visiting the logging village, Anson was shocked to find no church for the settlement of workers and families. Anson sent quantities of religious and temperance material to be distributed to the Phelps-Dodge employees. Their physical welfare was watched over and Phelps-Dodge Company built stores and boardinghouses near the sawmills.

By 1840, Phelps-Dodge had constructed a church, and Anson and William assisted in its dedication as the Presbyterian Church of Manchester. The design of the frame building was modeled after the Connecticut church attended by William's father, David Lowe Dodge. That same year the mill settlement in Tioga County changed its name to Ansonia to honor Anson Greene Phelps.

Anson engaged Hezekial Stowell as manager of the business for Phelps-Dodge. He then established the Phelps-Dodge lumber and sales center in Baltimore. Stowell served until 1851. E.B. Campbell succeeded him and continued in the position after Phelps-Dodge renamed the business the Pennsylvania Joint Land and Lumber Company in 1870.

(History of Tioga County)

Entrance to Village

The Phelps-Dodge furniture and lumber business became one of the largest in America. But, after thirty-six years, and hundreds of millions of feet of lumber being sent to market for furniture and building materials, the timberlands were depleted.

20

The Phelps-Dodge mill settlement, named Ansonia, in Tioga County was just north of the mile-wide, forty-seven-mile-long, and 1,450-feet-deep Pine Creek Gorge, which is often called the "Grand Canyon" of Pennsylvania. Today, as a village, it retains the name chosen in 1840 to honor Anson Greene Phelps.

Phelps-Dodge continued to invest in many forestlands, in other parts of North America, including those along the new railroad constructions.

William Earle Dodge pursued his special extended interest in the railroad developments, which promised to be of immeasurable help in trade and distribution throughout America. The railroads incidentally increased the demand for construction metals and timber from Phelps-Dodge.

Anson's partnership meant that extra attention could be given to the Phelps-Dodge import and export business. It also allowed Anson to further expand and diversify his new company.

Chapter Four

NEW DIRECTION

Anson had become the most important trader of metals and cotton in the United States. His extensive dealings with pioneering industrialists served to increase his interest in metal manufacturing, and it was copper, and its alloy, brass that most fascinated him with their possibilities. He believed they were key to great manufacturing developments. In 1832, Anson was ready to resume his former typical pre-emptive style of business on behalf of his new Company.

Eons had passed since copper was first noticed in the residue of a fire pit. Brass, however, not only had to be manmade, but required a component of pure zinc, which is not found pure in nature. Isolating it by a vaporization process from calamine for commercial use was problematical.

By the year 1781 (the same year that Anson was born), zinc was in limited commercial use in England, where James Emerson was experimenting to produce brass in a fusion process. He used approximately two parts of copper with one part zinc. Then he adjusted the proportions, so the strength and characteristics of the brass produced could be adapted for different uses.

*

The accumulation of capital and surplus supply of copper, tin, and zinc put Anson in an ideal position to design a manufacturing division for his newly organized Phelps-Dodge Company. New York's neighboring State of Connecticut had been officially recognized by the 1787 Constitutional Convention as a manufacturing state; although at that time, manufacturing was little more than an idea of the American Colonists. Anson chose to search for a suitable location in Connecticut, his home state.

*

The passage of time changes almost everything, including the face of the Earth. The shoreline of Connecticut has surely changed and will continue to change. What residents see today is not what the native Americans saw.

About nine thousand years ago, a glacier passed slowly through Connecticut. It left a large mouth of a river emptying into the Atlantic Ocean. In 1614, the Dutch explorer Adriaen Block discovered land that he named, "The New Netherlands" (New York). As he continued sailing his ship, the *Restless*, along the coast of Connecticut, he discovered and claimed the wide-mouthed river as "The River of Roodenberg" (Housatonic).

The discovery of the Housatonic impacted heavily on the future life of the tribes of American Indians living nearby. They belonged to the Algonquin Nation and were named for their location on the river.

At Old Derby, where the river widens at the confluence of the Housatonic and Naugatuck, the tribe was named the Paugasett. At the narrows of the cove in Milford lived the Wepawaug, and near the harbor in Stratford were the Cupheag.

One of the original ports in the State of Connecticut was formed, in a settlement named Old Derby, at the convergence of the Housatonic with its tributary, the Naugatuck. Although the inland tide-river froze in the harsh winters, ocean going vessels came into port and a very busy trade of furs, grains, spices, fish and agricultural products developed.

At the Derby Landing, a shipbuilding industry began in the 1600s and continued until 1868, when the last two-hundred-ton schooner, the *Modesty*, was launched from the Hallock shipyard.

✱

Viewing east of the mouth of the Housatonic River today, one might wonder about the Connecticut coastline that is partially protected by Long Island. From the Gulf Beach in Milford, and from other areas of the coast, there is a clear view of Long Island's Port Jefferson. When the tide begins to ebb at Silver Sands in Milford, a high sandbar begins to be dramatically exposed. It extends about a mile, connecting the shoreline with Charles Island, and stimulates wonder and awe about the power of the ocean and weather that changes boundaries of land and sea. Equally awesome is nature's power over mankind when, with sublime motivation, it engenders the vision and strength necessary for him to pursue a goal.

Many explorers have been lured to document or illustrate Nature's beauty. One such explorer was Professor Timothy Dwight, a famous educator, theologian, and president of Yale College from 1795 until his death in 1817. He wrote about his travels in New England and New York.

Dwight set out from New Haven in 1811 to explore and record his impressions of the Housatonic River and New York's Hudson River. Entering Old Derby from a hill, he saw where the Housatonic converges with its Naugatuck River tributary. He described the navigable Housatonic with its small island. There were vessels docked at the Derby Port wharves, and houses and stores near the Derby-Huntington Landing. The more distant Naugatuck River was noted as it wound through the beautiful rolling hills.

Thirty-eight years later, in 1849, Artist Calvin Curtis also captured the convergence in a painting. That was long after Anson, as a trader, became very well acquainted with that Port of Derby. (In fact the painting also captured Anson's 1834 Birmingham copper mill.)

In 1830, Anson had answered the call of colonists in Waterbury, seventeen miles north on the Naugatuck tributary. They urgently needed supplies of metals and fuel. The Waterbury area was proving to be a disappointment agriculturally and the settlers were desperate for an alternative means of survival. Some leaders were experienced in English metal manufacturing and worked to fashion old metal articles into buttons.

Their plan was to replace the customary wooden buttons of America and compete with those being imported from England. They needed investors. One of the most discouraging of obstacles was the unavailability of enough fuel for power. An annealing furnace required more than eighteen thousand cords of wood a year. Somehow Waterbury managed to establish two button factories between 1820 and 1830. Then, some industrialists in England were willing to invest in the area. At that point the problem of acquiring a steady supply of fuel and metal became urgent.

Anson set out with horse teams laden with the necessary materials. He experienced great difficulty in managing the weight of the metal and fuel over the

muddy or frozen roads from New York to Waterbury. He
tried sailing his schooner, loaded with supplies, as far as
the Derby Port, but in the harsh New England winters,
the rivers froze. Undaunted, he transported his metals
across the ice to the new factory by using horse drays.
The vital importance of acquiring not only metals, but
also an adequate source of power for manufacturing,
was deeply impressed upon him.

In 1832, Anson G. Phelps made his first capital
investment in the Naugatuck Valley. He met Israel Coe,
a Waterbury industrialist, and as a capitalist, Anson
joined Coe and a few others in a factory partnership at
Walcottsville (Torrington). There, the partners planned
to produce kettles by the battery method, which meant
hammering them from brass blanks, instead of using
the casting method.

The cost and difficulty of getting skilled workers
from England and the fact that kettles produced in this
manner tended to leak caused frustration among the
men. Anson disassociated himself and built his own
small mill, calling it the Ansonia Brass and Battery
Company. Just as his difficulties with the process were
surmounted, H.W. Hayden of the Waterbury Scoville
Company invented a greatly superior method.

The hammering method for making kettles was
replaced by the spinning method. Anson changed
his business focus and gave up on investing in kettle
manufacturing.

During this exploratory time there was
apprehension and opposition to Anson's interest in
manufacturing. Some of his family and business
associates felt he should be satisfied with his remarkably
successful trade business. However, Anson Greene
Phelps, a quiet man, was a great thinker. When he
made up his mind about the wisdom of balancing the
future of his company by diversifying, his decision was

as though written in stone. When the idea of investing in manufacturing had matured, he was immune to all objections. He would continue his search for an ideal opportunity.

Chapter Five

BIRMINGHAM

In 1833, while on his search for a satisfactory investment, Anson happened to meet Sheldon Smith at the Derby Port. Sheldon was an industrialist who had returned home, fresh from business successes in New Jersey. He was inspired to help the local economy recover from the depression it had suffered since the War of 1812.

Sheldon had already established an area named Smithville, but was in need of an investor. He had a canal, reservoir, wharf, and a main street with shops and residences already in place. He invited Anson to join him, his brother Fitch and John Lewis in a partnership.

Anson invested in what became the Smith and Phelps Company, and the Smith-Phelps Copper Mill was constructed on the Housatonic side of the confluence in 1834. However, Anson's partners became deeply involved in a former litigation suit and had to withdraw from the partnership.

In 1836, Anson bought the Smith partnership and the name of the mill was changed to the Phelps

Phelps Copper Mill

Copper Mill. He renamed the settlement and its piece of land, "Birmingham" after the famous industrial settlement in England.

Fire destroyed the mill the following year, but Anson was so encouraged by its early success, he rebuilt and decided to enlarge the area of Birmingham north along the Westside of the Naugatuck River.

News of his plan spread and a man named Squire Stephen Booth seized the opportunity and purchased a key desirable section of the Basset Farm that was located near the present Atwater and Clifton Avenues of Derby and Ansonia. The Squire planned to resell the land to the wealthy investor.

When the transaction began, Booth started bargaining over the price by raising it in increments of five thousand dollars. Confidently, he kept dickering in poor faith with Anson's emissary Peter Phelps, his nephew and the son of his brother Thomas, until the figure became thirty thousand dollars.

The Phelps sensibilities stiffened and the overly ambitious Squire Stephen Booth was left alone with both his land and the bitter ill will of his community over the loss of an important opportunity.

Determined, Anson summoned the Scotsman, John Clouse, his surveyor-engineer, and instructed him, "Find the best place in America for a manufacturing settlement, no matter how long it takes!" The Phelps Copper Mill in Birmingham continued to prosper.

✱

Anson supplied metals to mill owners in New York, New Jersey and Connecticut, and was in the habit of volunteering his business and organizational expertise, if needed. He became well known and made many friends, who were interested in his Birmingham settlement.

One such friend was Dr. John Ireland Howe, a medical man, who had observed the difficult work being done by people struggling to make pins in the almshouses of New York.

Howe was inspired to design a machine that would make a better quality pin and at the same time, eliminate the tedious work. Pins are often taken for granted, as are most inventions that have simplified former problems of everyday living.

Things have always needed to be fastened together. Originally, thorns from a thicket or wooden skewers were used as fasteners. In the days of the Roman Empire, bronze pins were made by hand. During the reign of King Henry VIII of England, more delicate and refined brass pins were imported from France. Such pins were considered treasures and sold at high prices in small packets.

It was indeed a long step to develop pins made by machinery, but Dr. Howe was determined to do just

31

(Derby Historical Society)
Dr. John Ireland Howe

that. By 1831, he had invented his machine and was intent upon starting production.

He founded the Howe Manufacturing Company in New York in 1835, but was disappointed with his pins. He consulted Anson who thought he might have better luck if he changed from using iron wire to a brass wire. He invited him to move his company to Birmingham and use his brass wire.

Howe accepted the invitation and relocated. An expert was needed to draw customized brass wire from the copper mill's smelted metal. Anson knew just such a man, and recommended Thomas Wallace from Manchester, England to John Howe.

✱

Thomas Wallace arrived at the Derby Dock with his wife, seven sons, and all their worldly possessions. It would prove to be an important day for the future of the Naugatuck Valley.

There were many difficult problems to solve at the Howe factory. The most troublesome was the perfecting of a reliable head. When that was finally solved, production began.

The pins Dr. Howe's machine produced were not only first quality, but also so affordable that they became "common." Success at the Howe factory demonstrated that adapting brass was key to producing results superior to iron. It reinforced Anson's belief that his pursuit of copper and brass manufacturing was worthy of development.

Other pin companies sprang up and began to compete with Howe, but most had to merge to survive. Howe had more than one competitive edge over them. He had also invented and patented a separate sticking-machine that stuck the pins into packets.

Moreover, in 1903 his company made history when it began rewarding employees a bonus equal to the interest earned on their yearly salaries. Other manufacturers took notice that, in times of growing unrest in most factories, Howe's employees stayed loyal. He set an important precedent for employers and employees. In 1908, Howe Company was sold to the Plume & Atwood Company of Waterbury.

The Howe Pin Machine is now in the Smithsonian in Washington, D.C., and the Dr. Howe residence on Caroline Street in Downtown Derby has been restored by the Derby Historical Society.

There are several streets in Downtown Derby that were named for the people of its Birmingham past.

(Derby Historical Society)
Howe Pin Machine

Caroline Street was named in honor of the daughters of John Howe and Anson Phelps; Anson and Olivia Streets, were named after the Phelps parents and their namesake children; Minerva Street was named in honor of a daughter of Sheldon Smith; and Elizabeth Street, for a daughter of Anson Phelps and another of Sheldon Smith.

Chapter Six

PROJECT DELAYED

One year after Anson changed the name of Smithville to Birmingham, President Jackson demanded that all land accounts be settled in cash. His edict struck a devastating blow to American business and the "Panic of 1837" ensued. The calculated profitability of Anson's Birmingham Copper Mill was not affected by the edict. However, it coincided with a bad decision made by the trusted manager of his South Carolina cotton business.

In addition, Phelps-Dodge partnerships with several of the merchants and brokers in Louisiana failed. A fifty-thousand dollar loss was incurred before those partnerships were terminated. Then, the Phelps-Dodge Company losses doubled and tripled.

Anson was forced to concentrate on his New York trading business and to divert his attention away from Connecticut. Close to ruin, he wrote in his diary of being haunted by the memories of his childhood days in poverty and despair, when his mother let him "cry for his share of bread."

Before long, his faith in the future resurfaced. He thought of when he was rescued by the church minister and taught the tenets of faith as a child. He rededicated his energies to keeping his "Covenant with the Lord" and vowed to concentrate on helping his fellowman to a greater degree, if the Good Lord allowed him to recover his losses.

1837 was also the year his daughter Caroline married James Boulter Stokes, the brother of Josiah, who died in the Phelps-Peck warehouse disaster. James ran a dry good business with his father, a wealthy merchant and an ordained minister. Providentially, this new son-in-law was in a position to offer help to Anson. With his own financial backing and assistance, he facilitated a bank loan at ten-and-one-half percent interest.

Anson then changed his company name from the Phelps-Dodge Company to the Phelps-Dodge and Company. In the reorganization, he retained forty-seven percent and allocated twenty percent for each of the two sons-in-law, William Dodge and James Stokes. The balance of thirteen percent he gave to his only son, Anson Jr., who did not share his father's enthusiasm for business. In fact his lifestyle was a vexation for most of the lifetime of Anson Sr.

Anson proceeded doggedly with his new company, but it was a delay of years before he could recoup his losses and return to investing in the Naugatuck Valley. During that interim, Anson's enthusiasm for developing copper and brass for his business and for the general economy of the immigrant settlers had increased. He felt the timing of adding manufacturing to his Phelps-Dodge Company was even better.

In his absence, more industrialists and skilled workers from Birmingham, England had settled in Connecticut; and the chances of finding employees had improved. With experience and confidence, he was primed to test his talents and tenacity of purpose in his renewed venture.

The generation of cottage-bred manufacturers and the cosmopolitan business capitalist were about to meet at a crossroads in manufacturing history. Copper and brass were about to approach a new pinnacle of development.

PART II

ANSONIA

Ansonia, Connecticut

Chapter Seven.

FOUNDING THE VILLAGE

Early in 1844, John Clouse met Anson at the Derby Port and declared he had ended the search for "the finest place in the western world to establish a manufacturing village."

Anticipating good news at last, Anson followed and wondered as Clouse brought him to a place a short distance northeast of the Derby Port. It was on the Naugatuck River tributary of the confluence with the Housatonic, opposite from where his Birmingham copper mill was located. Together they stood at the top of a cliff overlooking the Lower Naugatuck River Valley and Anson gazed at the panorama of possibilities.

A small dam was located in a portion of the river, north of an expanse of level meadowlands. Water could easily be diverted to a canal for additional factories erected away from the river.

Excited by the prospect of finally creating his village, Anson left to arrange the purchase of the

Kinneytown Dam from its owner, Raymond French of the neighboring town of Humphreysville (Seymour).

(Derby Historical Society)

Kinneytown Dam,
Canal Reservoir, and Railroad
1848

Anson's talent for evaluating people usually served him well and on this venture he wanted the best millwright and master mechanic that he could find. He recalled meeting Zeba and Almon Farrel, a father and son millwright team, in Waterbury. They had an excellent reputation for setting up various kinds of mills statewide.

The forty-four year old son, Almon, was exactly the person Anson wanted on his team to help construct his canal and the superstructure of his mill. Almon was pleased to accept Anson's generous contract and brought with him his own young son, Franklin, as an apprentice.

Clouse immediately prepared a survey to include ample residential and agricultural support around what would be the manufacturing district near the river and proposed canal. Sixteen-year-old Franklin Farrel assisted him and carried the surveying chain.

(*Commemorative of Ansonia City Charter*)

Franklin Farrel

(As a young man)

Anson arranged the purchase of parcels of land. A meeting was held in the Elizabeth Street, Birmingham home of Dr. Ambrose Beardsley, a respected leader in the greater community. The subject for discussion among the influential residents was the naming of the new village. "Phelpsville" came under consideration, but the English settlers objected to the suffix "ville," with its French connotation and the name had been used elsewhere.

Dr. Beardsley, versed in Latin and the leader of the discussion, suggested they use the Latin version of Anson, the founder's Christian name. By unanimous vote and with Anson's pleasure, the manufacturing village was named "Ansonia."

Anson planned to shunt some of the water from the Kinneytown Dam, southeast to a canal and holding reservoir. Then to construct a control station for the canal, at the north end of the village, at the end of what was called Liberty Street.

He designed the canal to run parallel along the river and cross under the Main Street of the village at the foot of what would be called Foundry Hill. Then, in back of the land on the east side of Main Street, the canal would continue along the base of the southern cliff, pass behind the proposed manufacturing center, and end at a millpond near Tremont Street Hill.

(Derby Historical Society)

Mill Pond
1898

Irish immigrants were the first to follow the English to Ansonia. They worked as laborers in the village, laying the streets and working on the canal. The manufacturing village quickly came into being between 1845 and 1846.

The constructions involved the combined dedicated efforts of master mechanic and millwright, Almon Farrel; master mechanic and engineer, Anson's nephew, Peter Phelps; and surveyor and master mechanic, John Clouse. Abraham Hubbell volunteered to join the team to help later, in case any of Anson's other contractors abandoned the project, which indeed they did. The underground sluiceways, huge water wheels, long drive shafts, belts, and turbines were put in place to provide waterpower for the manufacturing district.

Almon and his son Franklin erected the superstructure of Anson's copper mill on Main Street. That first factory of the Village of Ansonia was located at the present day intersection of Main and Bridge streets, facing the Naugatuck River Bridge. Anson named his business the Ansonia Manufacturing Company and made Sheldon Smith, his former partner in Smithville, the treasurer.

A state charter entitled the Ansonia Manufacturing Company "to manufacture and deal in rolled brass and copper wire, and in other articles." It was the first of many factories constructed on the canal and facing Main Street.

Copper and brass production of tubing, wire, kettles, and beds began. Following Anson's success with those items, sheet brass, sheet copper, brass door railings, lamp barriers, brass pins, copper rivets, burrs, braziers, belt copper, fence wire, and copper-bottom items were added.

(Derby Historical Society)
Ansonia Manufacturing Company

Between 1820 and 1850, thousands of workmen with families from Birmingham, England settled in Connecticut. Anson scouted around and created his workforce from the best of them. He used a three-tiered hierarchy, composed of business proprietors, such as himself; skilled English mechanics, such as Almon; and unskilled laborers, who learned apprentice-style on the job. The structure proved to be successful.

In keeping with the times, the first unskilled laborers were paid eight cents a day. By 1870, the standard pay for unskilled factory workers was the equivalent of $2.50 for a full day's work. The economics of the cost of living and monetary system based on the gold standard are reflected in these figures. Company profits were reinvested into expanding and strengthening the business.

People today seem oblivious to the fact that only very hard work by their previous generations produced a bright future for America. Only excellent leadership and work for little pay paved the road out of mankind's natural condition of poverty and hardship.

In 1846, during the first year of production,

under the supervision of Anson, forty employees produced 1.2 million copper products and, under the supervision of Almon, 300 tons of brass and iron products. The nine hundred employees of the village manufactured products worth over a million dollars.

As the number of factories grew, the village quickly began to fulfill Anson's vision. At the close of the following year, three woolen mills had produced 500,000 yards of cloth, 91,520 yards of cotton yarn, and 4,000 yards of cotton batting. Two paper factories produced 225 tons of paper, including the newsprint for the *New Haven Register*. Two other factories produced 100 dozen axes. Twenty-eight employees made 350,000 pounds of tacks and brads, and forty workers made 150,000 pounds of pins.

In 1848, Anson hired experienced George Cowles, from Walcottsville, to manage the copper mill. He continued to be in charge of that first Phelps-Dodge manufacturing establishment until his death in 1887.

The Phelps-Dodge import-export trading company supplied the village with raw materials and distributed its manufactured products. A Phelps-Dodge steamboat carried productions to the New York Harbor by way of the Housatonic River. When the 470-ton "Ansonia Steamship" returned to the Port of Derby, it was always greeted by a canon-fire salute and cheering from the valley residents.

"ANSONIA" Steamship

Chapter Eight

TWILIGHT CAME

Anson, as the senior partner of the Phelps-James Company, traveled frequently to Liverpool, England. He was making his usual January trip in 1853, when he suffered a stroke. He returned home and recovered enough to enjoy spending time with the young members of his family. His health was improving, when an invitation came for him to attend a director's meeting of the Naugatuck Valley Railroad.

The railroad had great importance for business in Connecticut's Naugatuck Valley, and in the past, Anson and Timothy Dwight, the namesake grandson of the former president of Yale, brought successful pressure to have tracks laid from New Haven through Ansonia. As one of the directors, Anson was enthusiastic about attending the meeting and considered himself well enough to go.

However, it was a cold winter and the seventy-two year old Anson was still in a weakened state. He became ill on the way and had to return home. He developed pneumonia and was confined to bed. His only son, Anson, Jr. devoted himself to giving him personal care and solace.

Anson Greene Phelps

As a youth, the son did not share the expected interest in business. He left to go abroad and lived in several countries to observe and practice different cultures, and wrote vivid accounts of his experiences to his American relatives. Those accounts finally aroused family solicitude for his well being and in 1841, he was requested to return home. Anson, Jr. complied and in 1845, married the daughter of one of his father's merchant friends. More mature and sedate, he undertook an active role in the business. He surprised his family and assumed the mantle of serious religious living. No longer vexatious, he grew close to his father and gave great comfort to him in his illness.

On November 30, 1853, seventy-two year old Anson Greene Phelps died from pneumonia. On the day of his death, he transferred his shares of the Ansonia Clock Company to James Boulter Stokes, his son-in-law and a trustee of the Phelps-Dodge and Company.

Surviving Anson were his wife, Olivia, six of their eight children and twenty-four grandchildren. Burial services were held at the Mercer Street Presbyterian Church in New York City with Reverend George I. Prentice officiating. He was buried in the Phelps family plot at the Greenwood Cemetery in New York.

This obituary appeared in the December 1, 1853 edition of the *New York Herald:*

ANSON G. PHELPS, Esq., one of our most prominent merchants died at his residence in this city on Wednesday morning, November 30th, at the advanced age of seventy-four (sic) years. He had been in feeble health for some months, and returned from England, where he had been in the pursuit of health, a short time since.

To write the commercial life of Mr. Phelps would be to delineate the history of this city for the last half century, for he has been identified with the interests and institutions of this metropolis for that long period. Born in Connecticut, which has furnished so many of the enterprising men of New York and having learned a mechanical trade, we believe, Mr. Phelps in early life migrated to this city, and engaged in the pursuits of commerce.

He was for many years the senior partner in the mercantile house of Phelps & Peck, and subsequently of that of the present firm of Phelps, Dodge and Co. These firms have excelled as importers of block tin into the United States and other similar concerns in this country in the magnitude of their business in that line, amounting to millions in a year. They have also been extensively engaged in manufactures of various kinds, particularly in iron wire and other branches of manufactures from metals, also in the importation of materials used by manufacturers.

Mr. Phelps was for a long time one of the owners of and agent for the old Charleston line of packets and was otherwise engaged in the shipping business with England some twenty-five years and were among the few merchants engaged in that precarious branch of business who passed safely through every vicissitude, accumulating large capital to be employed in other branches of trade.

The manufacturing village of Ansonia, on the banks of the Housatonic (sic) river, in Connecticut owes its existence and prosperity mainly to the genius and enterprise of Mr. Phelps, who saw its advantages as a commercial and manufacturing site, and called the latent powers of the Housatonic at that point into action. At his bidding hundreds of industrious laborers, mechanics and manufacturers have found employment and many families have been made comfortable and happy by the creation of peaceful homes and the reward of skill, industry and labor. As a merchant Mr. Phelps was extensively known and he enjoyed a remarkable career of continued prosperity in his undertakings. His accumulated capital was constantly employed in enterprises useful to his fellow men, among which may be mentioned works of internal improvement, which he always encouraged and aided. He was a proprietor and director of many of our most prominent institutions, designed to advance the prosperity of New York.

As a public benefactor and Christian philanthropist, he was alike conspicuous, contributing largely of his means to those objects which commended themselves to his judgment and sympathy. He did not expend his money in vain and futile schemes for the abolition of negro slavery, but gave freely from his abundant wealth to the promotion of practicable objects of benevolence, particularly the Colonization Society of the New York branch of which institution he was President at the time of his death. Few if any of our citizens devoted more time and money than Mr. Phelps to the cause of colonization. He was the true friend of the colored man, and has often contributed when called upon towards purchasing the freedom of blacks in special cases.

In his manners and social intercourse, Mr. Phelps was mild, amiable, and unobtrusive. He had a wide circle of friends who were warmly attached to him, and his memory will be cherished by all to whom he was known, and who can appreciate the virtues, which adorn the character of a public benefactor.

When Anson died, he was a man of surpassing wealth, and left the greatest charitable contributions to New York of anyone up to that time.

PART III

ANSON G. PHELPS
LEGACY and PROGENY

Chapter Nine

ANSON'S PERSONAL LEGACY

Anson had suffered the disillusionment of an idealist. In his later years, he confided in his diary about his growing deep concerns for the life around him. He was greatly depressed by the cheating he found in business, the sinfulness of so many people, and the lack of humankind's close relationship with the Heavenly Spirit.

Lydia Sigourney was famous as one of the most popular writers in America at the time. She wrote these memorial verses about him:

> The cares of commerce and the rush of wealth
> Swept not away his meekness, nor the time
> To cultivate all household charities
> Nor the answering conscientious zeal
> To consecrate a portion of his gains
> To man's relief and the Redeemer's cause.

Anson taught his children to be aware of the needs of others. The marriages of daughters,

Elizabeth, Melissa, and Caroline to men of similar beliefs produced the seeds of his dynasty.

To assure beneficence in his twenty-four surviving grandchildren, Anson tailored his wealth to encourage their interest in philanthropy. He added this bequest to his will:

> I give and bequeath to each of my grandchildren, living at my decease, the sum of $5,000.00 to be paid to them when they severally attain the age of 21 years. This latter bequest I direct to be accompanied by my executors with this injunction: That each of my said grandchildren shall consider the said bequest as a Sacred deposit committed to their trust, to be invested by each grandchild, and the income derived thereof to be devoted to spread the gospel, and to promote the Redeemer's Kingdom on earth, hoping and trusting the God of Heaven will give to each of that wisdom which is from above and incline them to be faithful stewards, and transmit the same to their descendants, to be sacredly devoted to the same object.
>
> I know this bequest is absolute and places the amount given beyond my control, but my earnest hope is that my wish may be regarded as I leave it, an obligation binding simply on their integrity and honor.

Chapter Ten

THE ANSON G. PHELPS PROGENY

As Anson Greene Phelps had hoped, each successive generation of his family used their energy and the power of his accumulating wealth for important social, political, and philanthropic endeavors. *Noblesse oblige* in their hands wove great intellectual, spiritual, and social advantages into the fabric of America.

A focus on three of Anson's six daughters indicates they married men whose ancestors had attained prominent positions in business, religion, education, culture, commerce, politics, and philanthropy. The combined descendants of Elizabeth, Melissa, and Caroline, actively engaged in the work of Phelps-Dodge and promoted philanthropic interest in the mental, physical, and spiritual well being of others, here and abroad. They became benefactors of specific social concerns and made lasting pathways for philanthropic and public service.

*

William Earle Dodge, Melissa's husband, and Anson's junior partner in the first organization of the Phelps-Dodge Company had also vowed to help his fellowman. He became a stalwart champion of the freeing of slaves, and actively supported the new Republican Party in selecting Abraham Lincoln as a candidate for President of the United States. He became more involved in the party after Lincoln's election and in 1865, he was elected a member of the thirty-ninth Congress from the Eighth District of New York.

Under the presidency of Ulysses Grant, Dodge served as a member of the Indian Commission. However, he became so sickened by the corruption at that time, within the Bureau of Indian Affairs, that he resigned from public service, and pursued his social interests as a private citizen.

William was influential as the president of the Temperance Society, and also helped to organize, and expand the Young Men's Christian Association (YMCA). He served as its first president. He devoted himself to the founding of the Metropolitan Museum of Art, and the American Museum of Natural History. He was active in the work of the New York Historical Society, and maintained his prominence as a leader in the Presbyterian Church.

In his greater maturity, William Earle Dodge systematically donated his wealth to scores of schools, colleges, universities, and seminaries throughout the United States. Abroad, he supported the Syrian College of Beirut.

A bronze statue, now in Bryant Park adjacent to the New York Public Library, at 5th Avenue and 42nd Street, honors William Earle Dodge as a business leader and great philanthropist. It commemorates his eight-year term as president of the New York Chamber of Commerce. The inscription on the pedestal states it was erected by voluntary subscription under the auspices of the Chamber of Commerce of the State of New York in 1885.

(Sharon L.C.M. Kelly)
Statue of William Earle Dodge

After William's death in 1883, the Phelps-Dodge Corporation was left in the hands of its extended second generation, represented in part by Anson's grandson, William Earle Dodge, Jr.

Although young Dodge and Theodore Roosevelt were close friends, the interest and involvement of the Dodge family in politics did not resume until the next generation with Cleveland Hoadley Dodge. Cleveland was a Princeton graduate and became a confidante and financial supporter of Woodrow Wilson, President of Princeton College, and President of the United States.

✱

Cleveland's sister, Grace Hoadley Dodge, another grandchild of Melissa and William Dodge, was sensitive to, and disturbed by, the living conditions of immigrant women and children in New York City. She organized a club for working women and developed it into an organization she called the Association of Working Girls' Society. After her group merged with the Young Women's Christian Association, Grace served as president of the YWCA board of directors.

In 1880, she established the Foundation of Industrial Education Association to teach manual and domestic arts in public schools. With social reform objectives still firmly in mind, Grace Hoadley Dodge joined philosopher Nicholas Butler in 1887, and funded the establishment of the New York College for the Training of Teachers. When the school was moved to Morningside Heights in 1894, its name changed to the Teachers College and was made part of Columbia University. Grace donated years of leadership to her favorite philanthropies and left one and a half million dollars to them.

The high standard of education and the established legacy has endured at the college. Grace's brother funded the Cleveland H. Dodge Professorship of Education; and in 1998, the Cleveland H. Dodge Foundation underwrote renovations to the Grace Dodge Hall and the Grace Dodge Room at Teachers College.

In October 2002, William Dodge Rueckert, a great-grandson of Cleveland E. (Earle) Dodge and president of the Cleveland H. Dodge Foundation, became co-chair of the board of trustees of Teachers College. Throughout the years, he had served the college in several capacities, and had become the director of the YMCA of Greater New York.

Descendants of Melissa and William Earle Dodge added new recipients to the list of their long-standing beneficiaries. Scores of schools and colleges include: Princeton University, Robert College in Istanbul, Turkey, and The Syrian Protestant College at Beirut, now known as The American University at Beirut, an outstanding learning center for the study of western culture, and Christianity in the Arab world.

✳

Anson's eldest daughter, Elizabeth, married Daniel James, an upper New York State farmer and grocery merchant from Liverpool, England. Anson made him a junior partner in the Phelps-James Company that he created in England.

After a downturn in the metal trade business in England, Daniel James retired. Of Elizabeth and Daniel's four children, three survived. Their only son, Daniel Willis James, joined his cousins in America as a partner in the next generation of the Phelps-Dodge and Company.

Elizabeth and Daniel's grandson, Arthur Curtis James, became one of the world's largest owners of railroad securities. He controlled forty thousand miles of railroads in western United States.

Arthur's benefactions included: Amherst

College, Children's Aid Society of New York, Hampton Normal and Agricultural Institute of Virginia, Tuskegee Institute of Alabama, American Seaman's Friend Society, Society for Promoting the Gospel Among Seamen of the Port of New York, The American Board of Commissioners for Foreign Missions, The Board of Home Missions of the Presbyterian Church of the United States, the Union Theological Seminary, Newport Hospital of Rhode Island, the Christodora House, Presbyterian Church of the City of New York, New York Public Library, and Presbyterian Hospital of the City of New York.

✳

Anson's daughter, Caroline and her husband, James Boulter Stokes, spent the summer months from 1849 to 1865 away from their home in New York City. With family aboard, they embarked on a schooner from the East River in New York and sailed to the mouth of the Housatonic River. Then, just as Captain Block had done, sailed up the river to the Port of Derby.

There they were close to their established summer home at 65 Elm Street, in the section of Derby that became a part of Ansonia in 1893. Anson often visited Caroline's family. It was a family that grew to include ten of his grandchildren.

The Stokes daughters wrote about their vacations, picking berries in the nearby woods and spending days at the seashore in Milford. The Stokes sons were not as thrilled by the place, because their father, in fear of their drowning, thwarted their interest in boating on the Housatonic. The boys were also interested in fishing, but their father considered it an inelegant and cruel sport. Just riding and reading were not special enough for the boys. They felt it a dull way to spend a vacation. However, their father remedied the situation by promoting all kinds of ball playing, horseback riding, kite flying, and excursions to neighboring places.

One of their sons, William Phelps Stokes, was attracted to the neighboring city of New Haven and later became the first of the Phelps Stokes family to matriculate at Yale College.

Caroline Phelps Stokes, her mother's namesake, was born the year after her grandfather Anson had died, and her father had become the first president of the Ansonia Mills. Caroline was a lover of books, and dreamed of building and stocking a library for Ansonia in honor of her parents and grandfather.

(Derby Historical Society)

Stokes Summer Home
65 Elm Street
Ansonia

(Commemorative of Ansonia City Charter)
Miss Caroline Phelps Stokes

Thirty-nine years after the death of her grandfather, Caroline, with the help of her sister Olivia, established a library at 53 South Cliff Street in Ansonia. On the triangular tip of the property she purchased, she first installed a watering trough on the curb of its intersection of South Cliff Street with Cottage Avenue and Prospect Street. Its plaque dedicated it to the memory of her favorite author Anna Sewell and the book, *Black Beauty.*

(Derby Historical Society)

Black Beauty Water Trough

Caroline engaged architect George Keller from New York to design the library. Its foundation was made of granite from the Ansonia Quarry. The classic building was constructed of reddish freestone from Longmeadow, Massachusetts, and its roof was made of unglazed Spanish Tiles.

The dedication of the library in June 1892 was a social event hosted by Mrs. Franklin Farrel. Prominent socialites from New York gathered at the Farrel Tower House on North Cliff Street for luncheon, and then proceeded to the dedication by strolling up the elm-tree shaded sidewalk of South Cliff Street to the new library.

(Derby Historical Society)

The Ansonia Library
1892

On the right hand wall of the library entry, a metal plaque with three bas-relief images dedicates the library to the memory of "Anson Greene Phelps, Founder of Ansonia, and Caroline, His Daughter, Wife of James Stokes of New York." An inscription reads, "Whatever Ye Do, Do To The Glory of God."

In 1893, the year Ansonia became a city; Caroline formally gave the library to the city, with the provision that fifteen hundred dollars be allotted from the city budget for its maintenance. The fledgling city refused to accept it. The library remained closed; during which time several bids to move it were offered by other cities that would gladly possess it. In 1895, the city fathers finally agreed to maintain the library and it was opened to the public the following year.

(Derby Historical Society)

Olivia and Caroline Stokes
Ansonia Library Reading Room

＊

Caroline's other grandfather, Thomas Stokes, had arrived in America on his own ship. He was a pious man and a wealthy merchant. In England, he was prominently engaged in business, civic, and philanthropic affairs. He was also a noted theologian, and founded the London Missionary Society.

In America, Thomas Stokes was known as a financier and the first deacon of America's first Baptist Church. He helped found the American Bible Society, and the American Peace Society. His son, Caroline's father, James Boulter Stokes was a fine-goods textile merchant, financier, and real estate owner in New York and Pennsylvania.

James became especially interested in charitable work, after visiting Bellevue Hospital in New York, and discovering its deplorable, filthy conditions. He found women alcoholics from prison were entrusted with the care of the patients. Declaring it unacceptable, he became deeply involved in helping the Bellevue administration improve conditions. Later he held important administrative positions at the Eye and Ear Infirmary, and the Society for the Prevention of Cruelty to Animals.

*

With similar social sensitivity during his early years as a cotton merchant, Caroline's grandfather, Anson, had observed the plight of slaves on the plantations. Later, with the power of his wealth, he involved himself in the fight against the slave trade and was instrumental in the founding and colonizing of Liberia in Western Africa. He continued to give assistance to people of color on a far-reaching scale.

Caroline and her sister, Olivia continued with their grandfather's interest and became major donors for education in America's south. They helped the Tuskegee Institute, founded by Booker T. Washington; and, built chapels at Columbia, Tuskegee, and Berea colleges.

When Caroline died in 1909, she left a million-dollar trust for the Phelps-Stokes Fund to improve race relations and to support the education of Africans, American Indians, and African-Americans. She established one of the earliest philanthropic family foundations in the United States. Focusing on education, her foundation was responsible, throughout the ensuing years, for improving the lives of countless people of color. The Phelps-Stokes Foundation remains a lasting philanthropic legacy.

✱

Caroline's brother, Anson Phelps Stokes (1838-1913) was born in New York. In his youth, he left America to work at the Phelps-James Company in England and was made a partner in the firm in 1861. As the company's metal trade business slowed, he organized the Phelps-James & Company Bankers of Liverpool.

In the next two generations of 1874 and 1905, two more Stokes descendants were named Anson Phelps Stokes. They also became promoters of benevolent enterprises. One (1874-1958) graduated from Yale College and entered the Episcopal Theological School in Cambridge, Massachusetts to prepare for the priesthood. In 1900, he received his bachelor degree from the Yale Divinity School and an honorary master degree from Yale College. From 1900 to 1918, he held the positions of Secretary of Yale and assistant rector at St. Paul's Episcopal Church in New Haven. From 1924 to 1939, Anson Stokes was the resident canon at the National Cathedral in Washington, DC. In that role, he became more deeply involved in the cultural, ecclesiastical, and social issues of the times. He was also a trustee of the Phelps-Stokes Fund that his great-aunt Caroline had endowed.

Anson Stokes also concentrated on helping American Indians and Africans find solutions to their problems. In 1931, at a meeting of scholars at Howard University, Stokes presented a plan to edit a project called *An Encyclopedia of the Negro*. However, when the group voted a year later, Anson Stokes lost to W.E.B. Du Bois, who had also been working on the idea. However, Du Bois was later unable to finance the project and the *Encyclopedia Africana* was not published until 2000 in Ghana, West Africa. From 1931 until 1948 Anson Stokes wrote major reports on the activities and results of the Phelps-Stokes Fund. After that he authored the monumental three-volume set titled, *Church and State in the United States,* in 1950. It describes the history of religious freedom under the Constitution.

✱

In the next generation, (1905-1986) Anson Phelps Stokes, a 1927 Yale graduate, became a theologian and the Bishop of the Archdiocese of Massachusetts, serving between 1956 and 1970. As a trustee, he also dedicated himself to the mission of the Phelps-Stokes Fund.

✱

Another of Caroline Phelps Stokes's nine siblings lived a different lifestyle and some thought of him as the black sheep of the illustrious family. This brother, William Earle Dodge Stokes was flamboyant and notorious for being a self-centered womanizer. However, he did make a sentimental tribute to Anson Greene Phelps and the Anson namesakes in the family, by leaving a lasting landmark in New York City.

William desired to make his own contribution to New York by changing the two square miles of Upper West Side Manhattan into what he thought it should be. With passion, he began to alter what was once an Indian trail and described by *Harper's Weekly* as "a rocky desert of unpaved streets and shanties." He thought that as a part of the great New York City of America, it should rival the Champs-Elysees of Paris, France.

In 1885, he began by building brownstones in the area above 57th Street. Then he brought pressure to bear on City Hall to have the roads paved. In 1889, he purchased twenty-two parcels of land at the corner of 73rd Street and Grand Boulevard and began to build the area's biggest and grandest structure, "The World's Grandest Hotel."

The hotel was planned to be the tallest building in Manhattan. It was designed to have twenty floors with a nine-floor tower in the beaux-arts style of scrolls, brackets, balconies, and cornices that were popular in France. William chose architect Paul M. Duboy from Paris to design the structure. Then, he proceeded to interfere with Duboy's work every inch of the way. Reportedly, the architect suffered a nervous breakdown and resigned. When the hotel was completed in 1904 by Stanford White, it had seventeen of the planned twenty stories.

(Lake County Museum/Corbis)

The Ansonia Hotel

William Earle Dodge Stokes named the luxurious building, "The Ansonia Hotel." It was described as being larger than an ocean liner. There were 550,000 square feet for 1,400 rooms and 340 suites. It was complete with ballrooms, dining rooms, service and amenities, and able to provide for 1,300 dinner guests.

The building incorporated such novelties as elevators, and a system of pumping freezing brine through steel tubes in the walls for cooling the rooms. It also had a pneumatic tube communication system to connect the rooms, and a large recreational swimming pool in the basement.

The Ansonia Hotel was intended to be self-sufficient, which meant that it accommodated a vegetable garden, chickens, ducks, geese, pigs, and goats on its roof. The tenants could have fresh eggs delivered to them every morning. However, the New York City Department of Health saw fit to shut down the "farm on the roof" in 1907.

In 1895, at the age of 42, William married a fifteen-year-old Cuban girl named Rita Hernandez de Acosta. From that marriage, "Weddie" (William Earle Dodge Stokes, Jr.) was born. His mother divorced his father, and Weddie lived with, and was raised by his two aunts, Caroline and Olivia Stokes. By 1907, eleven-year-old Weddie began living at the hotel with his father. There, he and three teenage boys formed a club, named, "Junior Aero Club of the United States."

The boys experimented with model planes, but were not very successful. However, they were also interested in the idea of sending messages without wires and began to spend all their spare time working on that. They found other amateur wireless experimenters in New York and New Jersey, and the boys decided to dedicate the Aero Club exclusively to wireless telegraphy and telephony.

To support his son's interest, W.E.D. Stokes, Sr. called a special meeting of the Aero Club members at the Ansonia Hotel on January 2, 1909.

(New York Herald Tribune)
"Weddie"

On that day, the Junior Wireless Club, LTD was formed. Its roster included an honorary president, consulting engineer, council recording secretary, corresponding secretary, treasurer, vice president, and W.E.D. Stokes, Jr. as its president.

W.E.D. Stokes, Sr. acted as the director. All members became Charter Members of the "Junior Wireless Club, LTD." It was the frontier of wireless communication in America.

Eventually the United States Government became interested in the surprising progress the youngsters were making, and a decision was made to control their activity.

In 1910 Senator Chauncey Depew introduced a bill that prohibited amateur experimentation. It was the first bill of its kind to be presented to Congress and, except for an immediate response from the organized Junior Wireless Club, would have ended amateur radio.

Weddie was voted chairman of a committee to go to Washington to argue before Congress against the bill. With an irrepressible spirit and dressed in knickers and a cap, the teenager successfully made the case that amateur radio had the right to exist.

By 1911 membership in the Junior Wireless Club grew to such a degree that it changed its name to the Radio Club of America (RCA). Anson's fifteen-year old great grandson, William Earle Dodge Stokes, Jr. (Weddie) was a charter member. The Ansonia Hotel became especially attractive to musicians and writers because of its thick soundproof walls. It was dubbed, "The Palace of the Muses," and such notable patrons as Caruso, Stravinski, Ziegfeld, and Giulio Gatti Cazzas of La Scala, the new manager of the Metropolitan Opera House, found it most appealing as a residence. Innumerable artists and famous writers lived and worked in its luxuriously supportive soundproof atmosphere. The terra cotta walls protected the hotel to such a degree that a monstrous fire in a neighboring building only cracked its windows.

Inevitably, critics considered the exceedingly extravagant apartment hotel with its super-luxurious amenities to be part of a mad dream. The suites had no kitchens and the residents merely ordered service from a special staff that provided meals and whatever else was needed for their comfortable existence.

As years passed, the place began to assume a bohemian aura, reflecting the decadent culture of the times. Even professional athletes and notorious gamblers, reportedly found it an attractive place to do business.

When William Earl Dodge Stokes, Sr. died in 1926, he left the hotel to his son. In 1942 when metal of all types was needed to support the war effort, William Earl Dodge, Jr. enthusiastically made part of his father's inspired creation a wartime donation to the WWII metal drive. All of the hotel's wonderful metal embellishments, its seven-foot tall corner copper dome ornamentation, pneumatic metal communication tubing, and the steel cooling system in the walls were removed and made into munitions and other military equipment for the American troops.

W.E.D. Stokes, Jr. sold the hotel in 1945 to Samuel Broxmire. He proved to be a scoundrel, by absconding after cheating his tenants. He ended in jail, and the hotel was sold at a bankruptcy auction to a mortgage holder named Jake Starr, for the ridiculous price of $40,000.

Starr allowed it to deteriorate further and in the 1960s, the basement pool area was called the Continental Baths and reportedly catered to a gay clientele. The formal attire for parties there consisted of a black towel. Many now famous entertainers new in their careers performed there.

By 1968, the hotel had so deteriorated that the tenants banded together in protest, under the new New York Housing Code. The owner, Starr, was infuriated because their resident association had obtained a lawyer for the purpose of improving the condition of his hotel. Starr laid plans to have the place demolished.

It took Mayor John Lindsay, Congresswoman Bella Abzug, and a five-hour protest performance in the middle of 72nd Street, plus a petition with 25,000 signatures to save the hotel. In 1972, the Ansonia Hotel exterior was declared a New York Landmark, but Starr continued to let the inside decay, and allowed the premises to be used for the promotion of vice. When Starr died in bankruptcy, the hotel was again sold at auction to a mortgage company.

In 1978, it was Jesse Krasnow, with twenty-five investors, who bought the building. Krasnow loved the Ansonia Hotel and dedicated the following twenty-five years to trying to restore it. His hotel became the most litigated residence in the history of New York City, and by 1990, the desperate owner made a change and bought out the tenants.

Krasnow never gave up on his building and he continually worked to eliminate its staggering problems. By 2003, he successfully converted the New York City Landmark into condominium apartments.

The building is named simply *Ansonia*. It is the word originally coined in the nineteenth century to honor Anson Greene Phelps.

(Sharon L.C.M. Kelly)

Ansonia
2109 Broadway, New York City (2006)

*

A painting of Anson Greene Phelps, by the prominent artists, William Jewett and Samuel Waldo, was first willed to his daughter Caroline. Her grandson, Weddie, as an adult, donated it to the Simsbury Public Library. It is displayed with a portrait of Anson's wife, Olivia Egleston Phelps.

(Simsbury Library)

Anson Greene Phelps

❋

Poetically, an old map reveals that the present Simsbury Library is located on property that at one time belonged to Anson's father, Lieutenant Thomas Phelps Not far from the library is the First Church of Christ that was endowed by Anson.

(Simsbury Library)

Olivia Egleston Phelps

Also not far from the library is the Simsbury cemetery where Anson, in his maturity, erected a beautiful monument, in memory of his mother.

(Sharon L.C.M. Kelly)
Dorothy L. Phelps Monument

The monument stands high with a statue on top, depicting a woman kneeling and looking heavenward

(Sharon L.C.M. Kelly)

Top of Tombstone

The inscription on the tombstone reads:

Dorothy L. Phelps
Died in 1792
Aged 45 years
Erected To Her Memory by
Her Affectionate Son
Anson G. Phelps

The graves of Anson's older brother, George Augustus, who died in 1778, and his father, Thomas Phelps, who died in 1789, are close by.

PART IV

ANSON G. PHELPS BUSINESS LEGACIES:
CITY and CORPORATION

*Anson's manufacturing village of Ansonia
attracted men of sublime motivations and inventive genius.
As the City of Ansonia, it
continued to fulfill the village promise.
It created wondrous possibilities and a lasting
momentum for the future of mankind.*

*The Phelps-Dodge Company
adapted throughout the years, continuing to keep faith
with Anson's founding philosophy.
It became
The great International Phelps Dodge Corporation.*

Chapter Eleven

ANSONIA CLOCKMAKING

Ansonia gained a wide reputation as "the place where clocks are made," even though Bristol had 250 clock manufacturers at one time, and was the leading center of clockmaking in Connecticut. Ansonia's reputation began in the late 1840s, when Anson met with Bristol's clockmakers, Theodore Terry and Franklin Andrews, who were successful in making metal gears for their clocks and were in search of an investor.

Anson believed, as did his contemporaries, that metal clock parts would produce more accurate time keeping than the traditional wooden parts which were subject to warping and swelling. He formed a partnership with the Bristol Terry and Andrews Company, and in 1850 the company began moving production to a new factory in Ansonia.

Some of the clocks made in that period were labeled "Terry & Andrews, Bristol" with dials marked "Ansonia Clock Company." Others were labeled "Terry & Andrews, Ansonia."

The Bristol company sold its partnership to Anson

in 1851, and Theodore Terry ran the company. Clocks were labeled, "Terry Patent, manufactured by Ansonia Brass & Copper Company, Ansonia, Conn." and also "Ansonia Brass & Copper Co., Ansonia, Conn."

A beautifully painted "Ansonia Clock" with its brass mechanism encased in cast-iron, and ornamented with mother-of-pearl, was a highlight of the New York World's Fair in July 1853, just months before Anson died.

The year after Anson's death, his clock-company building was destroyed by fire, but rebuilt by Phelps-Dodge at the original site. During reconstruction, clocks were made at the Ansonia Brass and Copper Company and labeled with a picture of the destroyed factory.

Ansonia Clock Factory

Modern day antique clock dealers rarely find an "Ansonia Clock" that was manufactured in 1860. That year only limited products were manufactured and those were mainly clock movements.

By 1869 however, the Phelps-Dodge trading

company began to focus on the clock business Anson had left for it. The Phelps-Dodge access to an abundance of metal made it possible to make the "Ansonia Clock" of ninety-five percent brass, a tremendous advantage over competition, and also a profitable outlet for the Phelps-Dodge metal trade. In that year, Phelps-Dodge delivered 90,000 pounds of brass to the Ansonia Clock Factory and 83,503 clocks were produced.

Eight years later in 1877, when the company held a joint stock meeting in New York, Phelps-Dodge founded a new clock factory in Brooklyn, and Henry Davies, a Brooklyn clock-maker, inventor, and case designer was selected to be its president. The new clock factory was named "Ansonia Clock Company."

The new larger factory was completed and new machinery installed in the spring of 1880. Both Ansonia Clock Company factories were then in production. Clocks were labeled "Ansonia Clock Company, Manufacturers, New York, USA, Factories, Brooklyn, NY, Ansonia, Conn., United States of America."

Ansonia, with its 100 men and 25 women employees, produced an estimated $440,000 worth of clocks. The output of the Brooklyn factory with its 360 employees fell short the first year. Both factories paid their skilled workers $2.50 a day, and unskilled laborers $1.25 a day.

The *Hartford Times* and the *New York Times* reported that the Brooklyn factory was destroyed by fire on October 27, 1880. Phelps-Dodge rebuilt and then gradually proceeded to close the factory in Ansonia. By 1883, the company centered all clock administrative and manufacturing operations in Brooklyn. At that time the labels changed to "Ansonia Clock Company, New York, USA."

The following January, Phelps-Dodge opened

sales offices in New York, Chicago, and London. Two years later, the Ansonia Clock Company was offering 228 different clocks. During the Chicago Exposition of 1893, a display of a large model of the "Ansonia Clock" attained worldwide notice.

(Derby Historical Society)

Chicago Exposition Display
1893

By 1914, the company was producing 450 different clock models, containing Anson's original mechanism. Phelps-Dodge agents were in Australia, New Zealand, Japan, China, and India. Large quantities of clocks were exported to eighteen additional countries. A traveler to a remote region of central Africa reported seeing a native ruler proudly wearing an Ansonia clock around his neck as his symbol of royalty.

❋

It was usual to find large models of an Ansonia Clock installed inside municipal buildings across the United States. Consequently, the City of Dallas, in Ohio was affected when it was ordered to change its name, because it duplicated another in the same state and caused confusion for the postal department.

A committee meeting was called to select a new name, but there was difficulty in reaching an agreement. The evening hour was growing late, when Postmaster Samuel Light came to wind the wall clock. A member watched him and felt a creative idea strike. He suggested the name on the face of the clock. The postmaster enthusiastically voiced his agreement. There were no dissenting votes from the committee, and a third city in America was named Ansonia.

❋

The Phelps-Dodge Ansonia Clock Company in New York became one of the largest clock manufacturers in America. Then, between 1915 and 1920, pressures from competition increased and a decline in business occurred. In the 1920s, Phelps-Dodge sold the Ansonia Clock Company and its Canton, Ohio Dueber-Hampden Watch Company to the Russian Amtorg Trading Corporation.

The deal, made prior to the Great Depression, included sending workmen from Brooklyn and Canton to set up the equipment and train the Russian workers for eighteen months. It was Russia's introduction to industrial mass production. They planned to produce time clocks for their factories.

In the 1930s, the Ansonia Clock machinery made

its way back to the United States by way of Japan. The "Ansonia Clock Company" was last located in Lynwood, Washington in 1970.

*

Many people assume that clocks bearing the name, "The Ansonia Clock'" have been manufactured in Ansonia, Connecticut, but the patented name means that the clock contains the metal mechanism first introduced in Anson's factory in Ansonia.

When Phelps-Dodge moved the Clock Company to Brooklyn, New York, many skilled clock makers and clock-parts makers were left in the manufacturing village. They continued with their expertise and helped Ansonia retain its reputation as "the place where clocks are made."

One such worker was John B. Gardner, an immigrant from Bavaria. He arrived in this country in 1842 and at the age of fourteen began working at a New Haven clock company. Nine years later, he moved to Ansonia. Then, six years later, in 1857, he established the John B. Gardner Company, on Main Street, as a manufacturer of clock dials and trimmings.

Following success, he constructed the John B. Gardner Block, a large quadrangle of buildings with a courtyard at 93 Main Street. It was situated between the canal and Main Street, near the Cliff Walk. The large complex accommodated entrepreneurs and industries.

*

Arthur Bartholomew was a student at the Gunnery School in Washington, Connecticut, when his father decided he should withdraw from school and avail himself of the industrial opportunities in Ansonia. The young man began work at the Ansonia Brass and Copper Mill, and in 1872, he moved to work at the Ansonia Clock Company.

In 1881, he joined in a partnership with Albert

Phelps, from Forestville, Connecticut, a former superintendent of the Ansonia Clock Company. They organized the Phelps-Bartholomew Clock Company to manufacture nickel-plated lever clocks, and clock movements.

Their first factory was located at the rear of the Gardner Block quadrangle; but, when the Ansonia Clock Company's large four-story stone factory was vacated in 1883, they moved and renamed the Phelps-Dodge Stone Mill, the Phelps-Bartholomew Clock Works.

(Derby Historical Society)
"Old Stone Mill" – "The Clock Works"

The company employed ninety skilled mechanics and experts in the trade, and manufactured versions of innovative alarm and time clocks. The Phelps-Bartholomew Company, with agents in New York and Chicago, became a highly respected company. It was instrumental in establishing the Standard Electric Time Company. Arthur Bartholomew, a Republican, was elected the first Mayor of Ansonia in 1893. He put his business in trust and served two years.

Other clock manufacturers in the new city continued producing versions of timekeepers, faces, and other parts and types of clocks, including electric and standardized clocks. The manufacture of a variety of clocks became one of Ansonia's biggest industries, and for decades Connecticut led all other states in the value of clock productions.

Clock production had long ceased by the year 1995, when the Ansonia Renovation Project applied wrecking balls to the Phelps-Bartholomew Building that had been known as the "Clock Works" building, and before that, the "Old Stone Mill." It was the last of the original downtown Ansonia factories. Its land became part of Kingston Drive.

✱

The year after Anson died, his Birmingham Copper Mill was destroyed by fire, for the second time. Phelps-Dodge merged the company with the Ansonia Manufacturing Company and the Ansonia Brass and Battery Company. Then, in 1869, it added a new Phelps-Dodge building on Main Street under the name of the Ansonia Brass and Copper Company.

At the end of the 1860s, other Ansonia factories were producing such items as: files, fifth wheels, pins, lumber, veneer, paper boxes, bricks, corset clasps, harnesses, horse collars, whips, melodeons, fish poles, textiles, and lead paint.

Factories were spread in a continuous row along Main Street and the canal. The Phelps-Dodge Company held the property and mills of Ansonia as a part of the Borough of Derby.

(Derby Historical Society)

Ansonia Brass and Copper Company
1869

Then, by petition to the State of Connecticut, Ansonia attained its separate borough status in 1873. In 1889, it was incorporated as a town. The town applied for a city charter and in 1893 was admitted as the 168th City in the State of Connecticut. When city boundaries were redrawn, Elm Street in Old Derby became part of Ansonia.

Also in 1893, after a new bridge was constructed over the Naugatuck River, Old Derby was named East Derby, and Birmingham was named Downtown Derby.

The official seal of the City of Ansonia bears the image and name of Anson G. Phelps with the founding

95

date of 1844 on the inner circle and the city charter date of 1893 is on the outer circle.

(Ansonia City Hall)
Official Seal

During its peak manufacturing years, such a large proportion of copper was used in Ansonia that the price at which it was delivered there became its standard commodity quotation. By 1917, copper was priced at thirty-five cents a pound and the selling price of its products was determined by the cost of the metal used.

After World War I was declared, the government set the price of copper at twenty-eight cents a pound, and the cost of finished copper products was determined by supply and demand.

A crucible would be an apt icon for this cradle of manufacturing that was once called "The Copper City" and later, "The Industrial Heart of the Naugatuck Valley." The City of Ansonia, a stellar place fashioned by men of sublime motivation and industry, deserves to be recognized and honored by its residents.

(Derby Historical Society)
Ansonia City Hall
1901

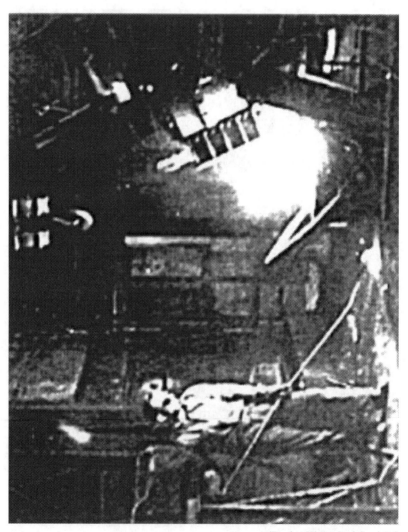

(Derby Historical Society)
Smelter at Crucible

Chapter Twelve

THE FARREL COMPANY

(Derby Historical Society)

Almon Farrel

Almon Farrel was the man Anson first chose to help establish his village. Later, Almon began following a dream of his own.

The village was rightfully named in honor of its founder, yet, as time went on, the Farrel name projected an enduring manufacturing profile for the city of Ansonia. Farrel's was the second factory constructed in the village, and its original office headquarters has remained active for more than a century and a half.

Almon wanted a special foundry for designing and manufacturing whatever heavy machinery might be needed for emerging manufacturing industries. There was a small factory in nearby Birmingham that was established in 1836 by the Colburn Brothers. It later became known as the Birmingham Iron Works. Almon had helped the owners with casting problems in the past, and they and the Farrel Company continued to be allies throughout the following years.

Almon chose four acres of meadowland along the Naugatuck River for his factory. It faced Main Street between North Main and Maple streets. Eventually his company acquired more property along the northeast side of the river and up North Main Street. Ultimately, the property extended east of the corner of Main and Maple streets, to the canal, and up the lower southern cliff. It included Union Street with its Victorian house, barn and coachman's house; to the corner of Union and State Street Hill, across State Street and to what would become his son's estate on North Cliff Street.

Almon and his young son, Franklin, began by organizing a machine shop named Almon Farrel and Company in 1848. It began producing power drives and gears for the installation of waterpower for factories and mills. He engaged Richard M. Johnson, an expert pattern maker, and Edward Lewis, a molder, for designing larger machinery. The company name changed to Farrel, Johnson, and Company and grew from three employees to seventeen hundred.

In 1850, the company was incorporated as Farrel Foundry; and in 1851, to supplement the Ansonia productions, another factory was constructed in Waterbury on the Naugatuck River named Farrel Foundry and Machine Shop.

Rolling mills for the brass industry were added to Farrel productions and in 1853 the name of the Ansonia factory was changed to the Farrel Foundry and Machine Company.

Farrel succeeded in making the necessary chilled iron rolls for its calender machines and their importation from England ceased. The first order for three calender machines to press rubber came early in 1854 from Charles Goodyear in Naugatuck.

(Farrel Corporation)

Calender Machine

Charles had accidentally dropped a piece of rubber, mixed with sulfur, on a heated stove, and discovered that the characteristics of the rubber product had changed. He named the new product, vulcanized rubber, in honor of Vulcan, the Roman God of Fire.

The India-Rubber Industry began ordering calenders from Farrel Company, and its periodical, *India-Rubber World,* reported that Farrel Foundry was the largest manufacturer of heavy machinery for rubber in the world.

Savoring success, Almon had "The Tower House" constructed on North Cliff Street as a gift for his partner-son, Franklin.

(New Haven Register)

Tower House

The estate covered the block of land facing State Street. The lavish mansion, at the top of Foundry Hill, faced North Cliff Street and the valley with the Farrel Foundry below. It always had the newest conveniences installed, and was remodeled many times.

Almon Farrel was given the title of "Founder of the Rubber Industry of America" in 1856. His machinery had made the industry possible. His dream of promoting industry, by devising the heavy machinery needed, had become a reality.

Tragically, in 1857, Almon Farrel died from a septic sore throat. He was fifty-seven years old. Following his death, the company reorganized under the name of the Farrel Foundry Machine Company, with Franklin in control of the family business and the manufacturing in the hands of professionals. The Company continued making large and small new industries possible by providing Farrel-designed customized machinery.

In 1869, Farrel Company led with its design and manufacture of sugar mills. Franklin was the company president when orders came from the West Indies, including Cuba, for Farrel's 320-ton machines to grind sugar cane.

(Derby Historical Society)

First Section of Sixty Freight Cars
Delivering a Sugar Mill

Each sugar mill was so huge that to transport just one to the New York Port for shipment involved the use of sixty railroad freight cars. An entire hold of a freighter ship was needed for the voyage. To complete an installation after delivery required an entire year. As a result of the Farrel designed mills, the sugar business began to thrive.

Farrel productions were numerous and unique. The all-purpose metal rolls, known as "Ansonia Rolls," were forty-four inches in diameter and seven feet long. They were the largest rolls, made in any country for milling flour, iron, steel, brass, lead, copper, and other metals.

Farrel-invented calender machines, with their chilled iron rolls, supported the paper, rubber, and plastics industries. As the names suggest, the stone-breaker and ore-crusher machines were made to adapt materials for use. Special cranes were designed and made to handle the various weights of heavy machinery.

*

In 1917, Fernley Banbury, an inventor, and employee of the Farrel neighboring Birmingham Iron Company, founded in 1836, changed the original design of the mixer being used for masticating and compounding rubber. His design revolutionized the processing of rubber, and made the old design, being used by both Birmingham and Farrel, obsolete. The companies merged in 1927 and the merger was named Farrel-Birmingham (F-B) with headquarters in Ansonia.

Another important invention came from the Birmingham Iron Company where David Bridge, from Lancaster, England, invented an improved friction clutch for water wheels and steam engines. Later, his own firm, The David Bridge Company of England, arranged licensing agreements with Birmingham Iron; and when the inventor died in 1900, his son, David Jr., took over. In 1918, and again, in 1926, he arranged agreements, allowing the Bridge Co. to manufacture the Banbury Mixer in the British Commonwealth.

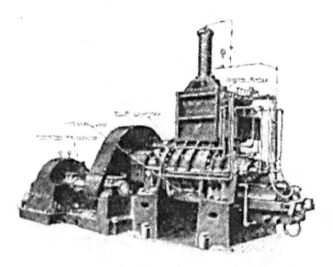

(*History of Connecticut*)

Banbury Mixer
1917

✳

In 1930, the David Bridge and Company, Ltd., of Castleton End in Queensway, England became the Farrel-Bridge Company, a manufacturer of modern machinery for rubber manufacturing and allied trades. The company went public in 1976 and became part of the renowned Emhart Group. Later, when Emhart sold Farrel-Bridge to the present Farrel Corporation, the company became known as Farrel Ltd.

Farrel foundries always supported our country's war efforts. In 1865, during the Civil War, it produced seven and one-half ton cannons. They were managed at the factory by Farrel-made cranes that used hand-driven controls. Ammunition was provided by the Phelps-Dodge Ansonia Copper Mill.

(Derby Historical Society)

Cannon Barrel

During World War 1, Farrel was busy making shell presses, gun carriages, and castings for the engines of more than 1,200 U.S. Navy four-stacker destroyers. By 1925, the manufacturing of foundry and machine shop products became Connecticut's second largest and most valuable industry.

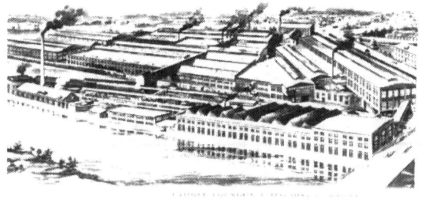

(Derby Historical Society)

Farrel Foundry and Machine Company

WW I

Farrel merged with the Birmingham foundry in 1927, its factory facilities increased in size and grew to cover thirteen and one-half acres.

During World War II, both the American Farrel-Birmingham and the United Kingdom Farrel-Bridge Company shared a patriotic focus. Farrel-Bridge made the machines needed for neutralizing enemy magnetic mines. It also constructed the machinery necessary for producing metal pipes to transport millions of gallons of fuel under the English Channel in time for the landing of Allied Forces at Normandy. Farrel-Bridge also made machinery to produce the plastic insulation, necessary for the electrical components of anti-aircraft guns, and rocket projectiles.

In Ansonia, Farrel-Birmingham produced molds for gun barrels and hydraulic presses for airplane parts. When the American Navy needed some ships to be powered by non-reversible two-cycle diesel engines to drive propellers through reverse gear, Farrel-Birmingham acquired the Buffalo, New York company that produced gears and gear units and secured the rights to the Sykes gear patents in an effort to fill the need.

Pioneering, Farrel worked to supply the reduction gear systems and equipment for marine diesels, and Farrel-Birmingham Propulsion Gear Units were available for the Navy in time to use on small seacraft, escort vessels, patrol boats, destroyers, submarines (and their tenders), mine sweepers, medium landing craft, tugs, and maritime commission vessels.

Farrel-Birmingham was awarded the United States Navy "E" Burgee Award for excellence, due to its production of the propulsion gear drives for Navy ships. It also received the "M" award for the excellence of its manufacturing. Fighting men, returning home, reported that seeing an F-B logo on their military equipment assured them of its quality and reliability.

✱

As Farrel-Birmingham grew in size and number of products, it purchased supporting corporations to allow adapting to the machinery needed to fill demands from around the world. Then in 1962, to comply with licensing requirements for manufacturing patented Farrel designed machinery abroad, the name Farrel-Birmingham was changed back to the private company name of Farrel Company.

The Farrel Company became known in England, Italy, Australia, and later, in Japan and India as Farrel Ltd., Farrel/Shaw Ltd., Farrel/Singapore, Ltd., and Farrel/Asia, Ltd. As a private company, Almon Farrel's Company had become enormously successful and rivaled many manufacturing companies in this country and abroad.

(Connecticut, The Industrial Incubator)
Franklin Farrel

*(Tercentenary Pictorial and History
of Lower Naugatuck Valley)*

Franklin Farrel, Jr.

By 1968, competition began to force the company to consolidate and limit its range of products. The Company had invested millions of dollars in the excellence of its innovations, engineering, and technological advancements.

Its systems engineering division was responsible for the design, supply, and installation of entire

110

systems and processing lines around the world. It also offered analysis, system maximization, and facility upgrades.

There were Farrel facilities on four continents and customer bases in more than fifty countries that were subject to the economic cycles of the plastic, chemical, and rubber industries.

Farrel's hallmark was its ability to supply changing market demands. As major market changes occurred, Farrel produced machinery to process sheet and molded rubber and plastic products, including footwear, wire and cable. Tire and rubber goods manufacturers later became Farrel's primarily customers.

In 1981, the Farrel family's active participation in the company ended with the retirement of its secretary, Almon's great grandson, Franklin Farrel III. The company became the Farrel Company-Emhart Machinery Group in 1983.

By 1986, commodity plastic developers were in need of Farrel machinery to process and compound their materials. A group of investors, that included Rolf Liebergesell and Alberto Shaio, vice president and general manager of the plastic division of Farrel Company, purchased aspects of the rubber and plastics business from what had by then become the Emhart-Farrel division of United Shoe Company.

Operating under the name of Farrel Corporation, the investors began supplying machines to the rubber and polymer processing industries worldwide. Farrel developed a new two-stage plastic mixing and compounding machine and introduced it at the International Tire Exhibition and Conference in 2000. The revolutionary machine was named the Farrel Ultima Compounder. It won the International Tire Exhibition and Conference "Trilogy Award."

*

Although the Farrel Foundry in Ansonia is closed, the office of the Farrel World Headquarters remains on Main Street. As the world turns, developing industries will need sophisticated rubber and plastics processing machinery. The legacy of Almon Farrel continues providing machinery to help industries.

Almon's great grandson, Alton Farrel, Jr., the son of Mayor Alton Farrel, was once an Ansonia public school student. He left an endowment to Rensselaer College for an Industrial Scholarship, with preference to be given to Ansonia students.

*

In February of 2007, the Farrel Corporation stockholders approved a merger agreement with its private investor group, and Farrel stopped trading as a public company.

At that time, the Corporation was described as a leading designer and manufacturer of machinery used to process rubber and plastic materials. The Company's products include BANBURY® and INTERMIX®, mixers, continuous mixers, single and twin screw extruders, plastic compounders, pelletizers, gear pumps, and mills. Farrel Corporation services includes repair, refurbishment and machinery upgrade.

(Derby Historical Society)
Farrel Headquarters

(Derby Historical Society)

Ansonia Main Street – (l-r) Farrel Foundry
State Armory, Baptist Church, Eagle Hose,
Farrel Office

Chapter Thirteen

THOMAS WALLACE AND SONS

In 1846, the same year Almon Farrel was beginning his foundry on Main Street, Thomas Wallace gave up his position as wire-drawer for the Howe Pin Machine Company. Equally intent upon pursuing his own goal, Wallace purchased property north of Farrel in the area of Liberty Street. He established a small brass mill to smelt customized copper and brass and improve the quality and technique of drawing wire. His dedicated work produced such improvements that, when accepted by the manufacturing industry, Thomas Wallace was acclaimed, "The Father of the Brass Industry in America," and in 1863, he was made the first warden of the Ansonia Borough.

With the help of his seven sons, Thomas constructed a brick and stone manufacturing plant that covered five acres of Liberty and North Main streets. In appreciation, he named the plant, the Wallace and Sons Copper and Brass Foundry.

Wallace and Sons became one of the largest brass foundries in the Naugatuck Valley and added to

Connecticut's record number of flourishing industries. During this time, Connecticut grew to surpass all the other states in the number of patents recorded.

Thomas Wallace

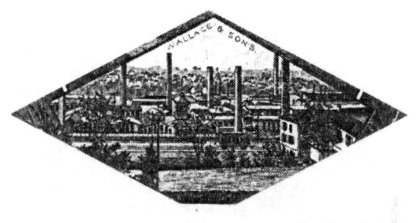

(New Haven Register)

Wallace and Sons
Brass and Copper Factory

Thomas Wallace, the "Father of the Brass Industry" had an interesting life with his seven sons. Six of the boys continued sharing their father's passion for developing the potentials of metals.

Thomas Jr. succeeded in improving on his father's technique of drawing wire. His techniques were such that they were officially adopted by the wire industry and brought him fame. William Wallace, another son, did not share the family interest in manufacturing, and outdid his brothers in provoking suspenseful interest from his father.

✳

To get a sense of William's pioneering days, you might imagine yourself being a teenager in 1876. You, a New-Havener, have been invited to visit your friend, John in Ansonia. To be invited on that particular day, it was necessary to be on the inside track with a close friend of William Wallace. Only the Wallace family and his friend, John, knew it was the day William was making a demonstration. With passion and determination, he had been pursuing efforts to harness electricity in the small workshop his father had helped him build at the southern tip of North Liberty Street, near the first Wallace Brass Mill.

On that day, you arrive from New Haven, by way of Seymour, and enter North Main Street. Not far from the entrance to Liberty Street, you are surprised to see John and a few others standing in the middle of the road. They seem to be staring at the western sky.

"What's happening?" you ask, and John explains, "I looked out my bedroom window, up there on North Cliff Street this morning, and there it was. We are trying to figure out what it is and how it got there."

"How could anybody get anything up that high? It is the largest and tallest chimney in the state, over two hundred feet! The clock tower way up on the side is eighty feet high. What do you think it is?"

One of the fellows hands you his spyglass. From that angle, you see an indescribable thing on the top of the chimney of the Thomas Wallace brass mill. You have no answer.

"I'm going to ask Will about it," John finally says, and leaves to visit the electrical shop. When he returns he is shaking his head, saying that Will is too busy to explain, but wonders if we could do him a favor.

"Will wants us to take a paper he has written and read it to his old friend on Division Street in Derby before nightfall." You walk about a mile with him to Division Street on the Ansonia-Birmingham town line.

After the introductions are over, you and John settle down to share what Will wants the elderly man to know. John begins reading. It is a treatise on electricity he has written. John barely gets started when darkness begins to fall and your host gets up to light a lantern. You hold it while John resumes reading.

Suddenly, the room is flooded with light coming in the windows. All of outdoors is brilliantly lit. You put the lantern down. It is definitely no longer needed to read by.

On the walk back to the East Side of Ansonia, you are caught up in something else. You discover that in Ansonia, it is the custom to arouse enthusiasm for a particular political candidate by marching through the streets at night with banners, and torchlights or lanterns. However, William Wallace was ready to make a difference for that year's autumnal presidential campaign of Hayes-Tilden.

You heard from a night marcher that when they were assembled on lower Main Street waiting for the signal to start, darkness fell. At the moment the signal was given, the marchers became as astounded as you, John, and your host had been when light flooded in the windows. The marchers proceeded on the brilliantly lit Main Street and rejoiced, noisier than ever in their wonder and exuberance.

You later learned how John's friend, William created his surprise. With a flair for attracting attention to his discoveries, he had inserted his many 500 candle power arc lights into locomotive headlights and attached them to the top of the Wallace factory chimney. The light flooded the towns. The excitement caused by William's invention was monumental. Ansonia became the first city in Connecticut to be equipped with electric streetlights.

✳

William wanted to use the 1876 Philadelphia Centennial Exposition as a stage for his latest inventions. The dynamo he invented needed to generate enough power for the event. He worked to meet the deadline and succeeded in lighting all of the Centennial Exposition.

The William Wallace invention was later put on exhibition at Columbia University among other scientific treasures. His carbon-arc light consisted of two plates of battery carbon fastened to a wooden frame. Later he used a metal frame. The light was able to burn for ten hours for ten nights. It was too bright for indoor use and later modified for lamps.

In 1878, because of wide attention that had been gained from the lighting of the Exposition, Thomas Edison made the first of several visits to "The Electrical Wizard" in Ansonia. He purchased two of the "Telemachron" eight horsepower generators Wallace had developed for his carbon arc lights.

Purportedly, Edison needed William's generator invention to light his New Jersey plant. Will's office boy, sixteen year old Franklin Silas Terry was present the day Edison visited with Professor George Barker.

At the end of the visit, he watched Edison use a diamond-pointed stylus to scratch "Thomas Edison, September 8, 1878, written under electric lights" on the wine goblet he used while a guest of William Wallace. Franklin Silas Terry was duly impressed and greatly inspired by the company of such men.

At the time, Edison could not solve the problem of contriving a satisfactory source of power for his incandescent light project. He used Will's generator as a solution. The next year Edison accepted full credit for his incandescent electric light invention.

In defense, Edison said, during a public discussion about the matter: "Wallace was one of the earliest pioneers in the electrical matters of this industry. He has done a great deal of good work for which others have received the credit; and the work, which he did in early days, others have benefited by largely, and he has been crowded to one side." Professor Moses G. Farmer, famous for his fire alarm system, was one of those others. He also worked closely with William Wallace.

(Derby Historical Society)
William Wallace Carbon Arc Light

At the 1879 America Institute Fair, William placed his arc light in competition with an invention by Charles F. Bush, who had also challenged him at the Mechanic's Institute Fair. Professor Trowbridge of Harvard made a comparative test of both systems and Trowbridge awarded the medal to Wallace.

William's father, Thomas anticipated the demand for electrical products, and in 1880, he organized the Electrical Supply Company with his son, to manufacture electric lights, telephones, and telegraph supplies. That year the *Willimantic Chronicle* in Windham County, Connecticut reported that slips of paper were found, tacked to the poles of the Rapid Telegraph Company, extending from Boston to New York, stating, "This line has been attached by Wallace & Sons Company."

✱

When the Wallace office boy, Franklin Silas Terry, graduated at the head of his class at Ansonia High School, instead of matriculating at Phillips Exeter Academy in Andover, Massachusetts, he chose to continue as an employee of William Wallace in Ansonia. He worked at the Electrical Supply Company in Ansonia until 1884 and then was sent to manage the company's new Chicago branch.

Terry excelled in writing in high school, and in 1892, he invested his own money to produce 5,000 copies of a catalogue he made, printed and distributed. It was a very successful promotion of the Electrical Supply Company. By the next year, the Wallace Company was the largest of its kind in America.

The catalogue listed the general office and warehouse of Wallace & Sons at 89 Chambers & 71 Reade Streets, New York. It stated that Wallace and Sons had been assigned at least thirty-five lighting-related patents in Connecticut, some of which were related to less intense lamps for household use.

Although Terry worked continuously for the Electrical Supply Company, in 1881 he used his talent for organization, and also helped to found the National Electric Light Association that banded together several independent electric companies. Then, in 1889, he founded his own Sunbeam Incandescent Lamp Company and was instrumental in consolidating small electrical companies into the General Electric Company, of which he became an official.

Franklin Silas Terry, this same Wallace office boy, who had achieved such success in the business world, was also a great humanitarian. In adulthood, he won the title of "The American Godfather" as a benefactor of World War I French orphans.

✱

C.D. Warner, another Ansonia inventor, was so fascinated by the telegraph-sounder that he worked on an idea he had for a new product. In 1882, he succeeded in making an electric clock that moved its hands once a second. He consulted electrical wizard, William Wallace, who offered to connect circuit wires to the clocks, if Warner would furnish the clocks and agree to keep them running.

Warner located some French electric clock mechanisms and Wallace connected them to a circuit that extended between the Wallace & Sons factory and the residences of its members. It was highly successful and became the beginning of standardized time.

✱

The Wallace Electrical Supply Company reorganized as the Ansonia Electric Supply Company in 1895. It continued producing magnet-covered wire, cable, and the new telegraph lines to be used across America. The Thomas Wallace businesses played an active role in Ansonia for 102 years, before it moved to Rhode Island in the 1950s. The manufacturing of electrical machinery and supplies became Connecticut's fourth greatest industry in value, and seventh in the nation.

The development of electrical power allowed some Ansonia manufacturers to locate away from the canal and river, and the number of small shops multiplied. With an outstanding array of industries, Ansonia differed from other manufacturing cities that were known for just one type of production. Ansonia, known as "The Copper City" in the beginning, was later referred to as "The Industrial Center of Lower Naugatuck Valley."

Some of the industries established after Anson's death include:

The Ansonia Osborne & Cheeseman Company, manufacturers of elastic webbing, shoe and corset laces, arm bands, boxed lisle elastic, hoop skirts, and brass goods; Wilcox and Terrill, fifth wheels; E. I. Bryant, hoopskirts; Cotter & Carter, brass; J. Jackson, iron; Charles Mansfield, pins; T.B. Smith, veneer; Steele & Company, paper boxes; Shipman & Tucker, bricks; J.H. Bartholomew & Webster, corset clasps; M.A. Brown, harnesses and horse collars; Fraher, harnesses and whips; Page Porter & Company, melodeons; and H.B. Whiting, fish poles.

The R.R. Colburn & Company, in 1872, became manufacturers of white lead & paint; M.I. Blackman began manufacturing tin ware and stoves; Hendryx & Bartholomew was providing paper boxes, and patented brass bird cages; and Cullen & Thomas, in the west-side residential area, was manufacturing files.

The production of lamps and special function clocks, such as alarm and standardized, began at the Phelps and Bartholomew Company, in 1881.

In 1882 Sperry Manufacturers were specializing in making carriage hardware. The Ansonia Novelty Company opened for business, in 1889, to manufacture various items of steel, aluminum, brass, nickel, and silver for sewing thimbles. Products included Richard spring-bottom oilers, screw machine products, metal stamping, drawings, and novelties.

In 1901, the H.C. Cook Company opened and became famous for manufacturing fingernail clippers, hardware, metal specialties, fishing gear, and steel and brass stampings. The Cook Company was not on the canal or the Naugatuck River, but on Beaver Brook where, in the 17th century there had been a gristmill that produced grains for the Derby Port trading station.

The Cameron Electrical Manufacturing Company was established in 1902, on Main Street, across from the T.P. Terry Building. It manufactured all classes of commutators and electrical parts.

The John B. Dearborn Company, located on South Cliff Street in a residential area next to Christ Church, manufactured chuck machine tools; and, across the Naugatuck River from Farrel, the Jockmus Company produced small tools.

A later addition to Ansonia manufacturing was made in 1975. The George Middleton Advanced Precision Castings Company purchased the 1890 brass plumbing foundry located at the end of the residential area of Pleasant Street. George made castings from his designs in aluminum, sand, and plaster molds for the plastics industry. Some of his products were used as containers for toys including "Happy Meal" for McDonalds. He also filled contracts to design molds for Estee Lauder perfumes, Revlon cosmetics, Bic lighters, and for such items as flashlight battery packages, cold cut display trays, candy box liners, and decorative art for the lighting fixture and toy industries.

Chapter Fourteen

"THE WOODEN HORSE"

Imagine the day you discover that the village of Ansonia is mainly a stage for men with new ideas. You arrive for a visit with John and his friends in the evening, and hear there is a surprise in store for you the next day. The call to "rise and shine" rouses you out of bed. But, as you are getting dressed, you pick up your shoes and notice they need more than just a shine. The thinly worn spot on the center of their soles will make your walk back to New Haven uncomfortable.

You take the time to cut out wads of the *New Haven Register* you brought with you and line the inside of the shoes before proceeding. As you hasten to join your friends at breakfast, you wonder again if you will ever manage the cost of buying and keeping a horse.

As you walk with John and his friends to the top of Foundry Hill, you see and hear a group of people gathered at the foot of its cobblestone road. The year is 1865 and there is not yet a YMCA, State Armory or Baptist Church on the hill and no Eagle Hose Firehouse at its bottom.

You stand with your back to the gate of the path near the white fence coming down from the house on the ledge of the cliff and face Farrel Foundry across Main Street. A few cannon barrels are near the loading area by the foundry driveway. They are part of a military shipment.

(*Derby Historical Society*)

Farrel Foundry
Gate at Bottom of Hill
1865

More and more people begin to arrive, and the excitement increases. Your friends say, "Wait and see," when you ask what the surprise is, and after a while you decide you have waited long enough. But, before you can insist on an answer, a cheer goes up from the area of North Main Street. "There it is!" someone shouts, and coming around the curve on the dirt road of Main Street is a contraption with a man sitting on top of it!

You stare at the "surprise." John explains that it is the new "Wooden Horse" invented by Ansonia residents Pierre Lallament from France and James Carrol from Ireland, and that this is the day of its final testing. You watch how Lallament dismounts and carefully examines the details of the working parts. Then, as he begins his test journey, you and your friends begin walking beside him. Quickly you start running to keep pace with its spinning wheels.

The village citizens lining Main Street watch as he pedals down to the covered bridge (later called the Bridge Street Bridge) over the Naugatuck River. He maneuvers left to the country road (Clifton Avenue) leading to Birmingham (Derby).

(*Derby Historical Society*)

Bridge Street Bridge

People waiting along the test route that day saw Lallament repeat the trip several times and occasionally dismount to check the parts of his invention. (Lallement's descendants later told of many longer tours of the Valley.)

Ansonia residents enthusiastically accepted the idea of a "wooden horse." Many were anxious to learn to balance and ride it. During one of his longer trial runs, Lallament was arrested for disturbing the peace. A team of horses became so frightened by the strange contraption, competing for space on the road, that they went out of the control of the driver. Head bridles to block the side vision of the horses were later invented, and probably contributed to the decision that covered bridges were no longer needed (since anxiety seemed not to plague the horses, if they did not see the water).

Lallament filed a patent for what he called a velocipede in 1866. It was the first bicycle patent in America. For a long time, local residents continued to call the velocipede, a wooden horse. Later, when bicycles were made of metal, some people continued calling those, and tricycles, velocipedes.

(Derby Historical Society)

Velocipede Patent Papers

Chapter Fifteen

"THE HORSE RAILWAY"

Ansonia was a magnet, not only for industrialists, inventors, and entrepreneurs of all types, but also for enthusiastic immigrants ready to be employed. It was usual to see Irish construction workers busy around the settlement.

If a visitor came to downtown Ansonia by way of the Maple Street Bridge in the late 1880s, he would have found Main Street a daunting sight. It was not passable. Men were digging, shoveling dirt, and laying metal tracks in the middle of the road. The scene was vaguely reminiscent of the first time tracks were laid in Birmingham to guide horses pulling special transportation cars. That mode of transportation spread to other cities, and was regarded as "the latest thing." The digging in Ansonia, however, was more extensive, and with the help of William Wallace, "The Electrical Wizard," the Ansonia tracks were the beginning of something that had never been seen in all of New England before. They were for an electric trolley system that was inaugurated in 1887.

(Derby Historical Society)

First New England
Electric Trolley Tracks
Ansonia Main Street

(Derby Historical Society)

Derby Horse Railway
Atwater Avenue
1885

At first the trolley car system was named the Derby Horse Railway. Later it was called the Birmingham & Ansonia Horse Railway Company.

In 1887, its rails began to connect east Ansonia with the Derby Docks for freight service. Soon a passenger service was added with tracks circling Ansonia, Old Derby, and Birmingham.

The Derby Street Railway took over the company and housed the trolley cars in a garage on Main Street, Birmingham near the area of the present Home Depot shopping complex. Then the company changed its name from Derby Street Railway to the Ansonia, Derby & Birmingham Railway. In the 1900s, the CR&L arm of the New York-New Haven-Hartford Railroad bought the service.

The trolley system added connections from Ansonia to New Haven, Milford, and Bridgeport, and afforded access to their beaches, for the pleasures of swimming, boating, and renting summer cottages. Perhaps more importantly, trolleys provided travel for students to attend colleges, and for workers, to find employment in larger cities.

Imagine that time, when all things seemed possible by exchanging a quarter for three tokens that included transfer connections to far away cities. The punctual electric "Horse Railway" facilitated many wondrous adventures.

The service continued until "progress" arrived in Ansonia in 1937. It came in the guise of petrol motor buses.

Chapter Sixteen

"THE IRON HORSE"

It was vital to keep freight service in pace with the manufacturers' output. Much more than trolley service was needed to transport goods to the Port of Derby. Innovations began for improving railroad service to New York and elsewhere from the Valley.

In 1868, the Naugatuck Railroad Company made an agreement with the New York and New Haven Railroad Company to run trains from the Naugatuck Junction in New Haven to Bridgeport and from Waterbury to New Haven. On August 5, 1871, the New Haven and Derby Railroad opened service to New Haven over the same line.

In 1888, the newly invented electric freight locomotive named, "The Iron Horse" began its initial run in Ansonia on the New Haven and Derby line. As usual with trials of new things in Ansonia, excitement was high. Many stood on the bridges to gain a better view of the railroad tracks. A test of three and three-quarters miles through Derby and back was to be made.

A description of the electric locomotive debut, with thirty invited guests aboard, was printed in *The Palladium* of New Haven:

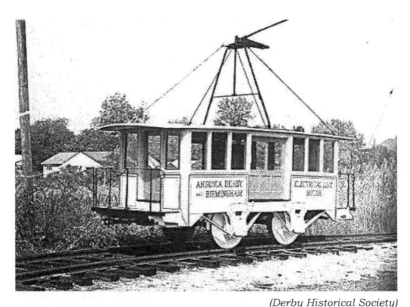

(Derby Historical Society)
First Electric Locomotive

"The Iron Horse"

The motor was a handsome cream-colored four-wheeled car, the sixteen feet forward car is partitioned off and in the compartment is situated the motor of about three or four horsepower. The motor soon struck a grade of a rise of about five feet in one hundred as it left Ansonia and around a curve of two hundred feet radius. It went very smoothly and nicely. When it came to Miller's Place, the rise was seven feet in one hundred and the car was stopped to prove that the engine could be readily started again. The plan was entirely successful. Through Derby, an even speed of twelve miles an hour was obtained and the test trip of three and three-quarters miles was made in about twenty minutes. It was proven entirely successful.

The "Iron Horse" was the forerunner of more efficient rail service for the distribution of products from the Naugatuck Valley to the Naugatuck Steamboat Company wharf at Pier 39 in New York.

Upon the occasion of the one-hundredth anniversary of that initial 1888 test trip, the original locomotive, stored at the Branford Museum in Connecticut, was returned to Ansonia for a festive celebration. People lined up to watch it retrace its maiden trip. This time, though, it had to be carried on a conveyor.

(Lower Naugatuck Valley Windsor Publication)
One-Hundredth Anniversary
Celebration in Ansonia
1989

In 1908, a double tracking of the Naugatuck Division Railroad was extended from Wheelers Farms near the Derby-Milford Turnpike to Waterbury. In places, the construction of the railway was very difficult because it had to span the Naugatuck River.

An entirely new railroad route was built from the Derby Junction in New Haven to Ansonia. It eliminated the former New Haven-Derby-Naugatuck railroad between those points.

Then, in 1912, another successful invention was tested and installed on the railway section between Derby and Ansonia. It was the first automatic train control.

Chapter Seventeen

EAGLE HOSE COMPANY

(Derby Historical Society)

Firefighters and Equipment
(Ladders, Sled with Hose)
Farrel Tower House in background
1870

Fighting fires was a challenge for the manufac-turing village of Ansonia. In that period, before modern fire-fighting equipment and techniques were developed, it was practically impossible. Wooden churches and mills were especially prone to complete destruction. In 1871, a meeting was held in the pristine one-year-old Ansonia Opera House to discuss the situation.

Among the assembled group were the influential successor of the Almon Farrel manufacturing business, Franklin Farrel, and his friend, William Wallace, the electrical genius. As a result of the meeting, twenty-five men volunteered to establish a fire company.

(Derby Historical Society)

Original Firehouse, and
"Jumper" Carriage

The company's building was constructed on North Main Street in August of the same year. It was the first fire company in the village, and today it remains the oldest fire department to retain its volunteer status in America.

In 1879, the original wooden firehouse was moved to Main Street and positioned over the section of the Anson Phelps canal that emerged from under Main Street.

Later, to accommodate the growing membership and more modern fire-fighting equipment, a larger firehouse of brick was erected closer to the road at the same address of One Main Street.

(Derby Historical Society)

New Fire Hose House
One Main Street
1905

The company name of "Eagle Hose Company #6" was appropriated from a brass plaque, found on the second-hand, man-drawn jumper carriage for hose equipment that the members purchased in New Jersey in 1871.

Throughout the years, that carriage has been used in patriotic parades, both in and away from Connecticut. The firefighters proudly pull the well-kept ornate "jumper" with its fifty-foot hose and impressive large golden eagle ornament at its top.

(Eagle Hose Company #6)

Parading Eagles

The Eagles were famous for their intricate and original parade drills that showcased their precision and teamwork. The drills were first practiced in the Opera House and later greatly admired for their interesting patterns. A signature drill of the "Eagles" was the highlight of long parades. Performed during the march, it consisted of their holding the reins of the carriage in their file, then drilling from a forward to side and reverse direction.

Originally the Civil War style dress uniforms consisted of white pants, partially covered with brown leggings, a navy blue jacket and a sharp brimmed hat. Later a more modern version was adopted. The Eagle Hose, Hook and Ladder Company #6 Parade Unit has always been the pride of Ansonia. With camaraderie, the well-trained volunteers share a passion for fighting fires, and their up-to-date, modern, fully equipped vehicles stay ready for instant action.

(Family Scrapbook)
Eagles' Uniform
Alfred Clifton Crossland

There is a golden eagle weathervane perched on top of the Eagles Firehouse Building that dates back to the Civil War. It was discovered in an antique collection belonging to the city's well-known salvage man, who had originally been accustomed to call, "cash paid for rags" from his horse wagon. Later as an antique dealer, he donated the weathervane to the Eagles.

The Derby Historical Society has chronicled the history of that eagle from the early 1850s, when it was on the roof of the Blackman building in Ansonia, across from the Boston Store at the corner of Bridge and Main streets.

Mr. Blackman, was a pacifist and not in favor of the Civil War. In 1864, "O Liberty, what Crimes are Perpetuated in Thy Name" appeared on the eagle's wings. One night, somebody climbed to the roof of his building, covered the eagle with a sack, and added a secessionist flag. The next day Charles Nettleman, a resident of the building, went to the roof with Blackman to remove the flag and the sack.

Residents of the hotel watched from across Main Street, and threw stones at them. Mr. Nettleman drew his revolver and the stone throwing stopped.

The incident upset Mrs. Blackman and her niece very much. They joined forces and spent the night knitting an American flag. Before the dawn's early light, the flag was flying and the writing on the eagle's wings had changed to "Victory to the Peacemakers." Without embellishments, that golden eagle weathervane now remains high on the roof of the "Eagle Headquarters" at One Main Street.

The Eagles building covered a section of Anson's canal as it exited from under Main Street. The canal continued out from under the back of the building and a metal rail fence followed its course as it bordered the

Farrel Pattern Shop driveway. The canal continued past the line of factories to the millpond near Tremont Street Hill.

(Derby Historical Society)
Eagle on Blackman Building
(Corner of Main and Bridge Streets)

After the 1955 hurricanes and flood, plans were made to remove the vestiges of the closed, obsolete canal from under the firehouse. On July 31, 1957, the tailrace channel that led from the huge water wheel of the canal under Main Street was sealed. The visionary firefighters claimed the space as its cellar and built an activity room aptly named, "The Canal Room."

The Farrel Company and family were steadfast supporters of the Eagle Hose Fire Department. Many employees were Eagle firefighters and were allowed to leave work to respond to all fire alarms.

The large tower bell on Farrel's Main Street Foundry had been used during the last half of the 19th century to signal lunchtime. It remained in the tower of that building, long after an electric whistle replaced it. A day came in 1964, when Farrel had the traffic on upper Main Street stopped while the bell was dismounted. It was donated to the Eagle Hose Company and positioned on the lawn at the side of the firehouse, facing Main Street and the Farrel Foundry building.

(Derby Historical Society)

Memorial Bell

(Derby Historical Society)

Removing the Bell
1964

Chapter Eighteen

THE EVENING SENTINEL

Another important event took place in 1871. Reverend Jerome, a Baptist minister, whose church was about to be constructed near the foot of State Street's Foundry Hill, planned to publish the first Valley newspaper in a building near the top of the hill.

When the publication began, it was a four-page weekly edition named, *The Naugatuck Valley Sentinel.* Soon a larger facility was needed, and Reverend Jerome moved the business to the building on the corner of Main and Maple streets, across from the First Methodist Episcopal Church.

By 1876, Jerome's *Naugatuck Valley Sentinel* was well established. He sold the business to J. Marion Emerson, who ran it as a family-owned business. It was the printing era of setting lead type by hand and using a flatbed press. As soon as linotype machines were invented, Mr. Emerson eagerly purchased the first of the five available. By 1901, *The Naugatuck Valley Sentinel* had the highest per capita circulation of any newspaper in Connecticut. When it grew into a daily edition, it was renamed *The Evening Sentinel.*

The edition covered the local news, of Ansonia, Derby, Seymour, Shelton, Oxford, and Beacon Falls. The publishing company of Emerson and Brothers became one of the first clients of the Associated Press telegraphic news in the area, and added world news to the publication.

On exciting election nights in the 1920s, the *Sentinel* projected running voting tallies, as soon as reported, from a window on the second floor of the T.P. Terry Building to the wall of the Cameron Electric Factory across Main Street, while enthusiastic voters watched.

The carefully read first page of *The Evening Sentinel* gave the headline news of the world and of area towns. Many anxious or curious readers skipped that part to look first at the center bottom, where the local obituary, birth, and marriage news was printed. Remarkably correct weather forecasts were given without sophisticated weather-predicting technology. The weather box, placed at a top corner of the first page usually predicted "partly cloudy" or "partly sunny," and was rarely wrong. It seems that even the weather was better when predicted by *The Evening Sentinel.*

Newspaper boys delivered editions over all the area towns. Some rode bicycles, and some walked, with or without a clever dog trained to help. *The Sentinel* never missed a day of its publishing schedule. Editions were put out throughout such disasters as the Blizzard of 1888, the Hurricane of 1938, and the Flood of 1955 (that inundated downtown with a water level mark at eight feet on the Sentinel building next to City Hall). That Naugatuck River flood was caused by the combination of two disastrous hurricanes, Connie and Diane. It undermined the railroad tracks along the river and a freight car, waiting on the track spur at Farrel Foundry, was displaced. The American Brass Company's private bridge became detached and floated away. It added to other debris in the river that crashed into, and demolished, the two bridges that connected the east and west sides of Ansonia. Water supply conduits under the river were damaged and the Westside of Ansonia was without potable water.

Manufacturing establishments, downtown businesses, homes, and churches were damaged or destroyed. The roof of the Capitol Theater became a landing pad for helicopters to make heroic rescues of stranded people. *The Evening Sentinel* had plenty of material and pictures to publish for days.

The newspaper continued as a vibrant institution in the Valley until 1969. Then, without previous notice, the great-granddaughter of J.M. Emerson sold the paper to the Illinois conglomerate, Thomson Newspapers, Inc., and publication ceased abruptly on Christmas Eve. The upsetting turn of events was deeply felt by the *Sentinel's* loyal employees and readers. The towns were left without their familiar local and worldly newspaper.

In the year 2000, the cities of Ansonia, Derby, Shelton, Seymour, and Beacon Falls, those the *Evening Sentinel* had provided with current news, were collectively designated as an "All-American City."

It was a bittersweet honor that recognized that an era had passed in the Lower Naugatuck Valley. The beloved *Evening Sentinel* could not publish news of the award.

Chapter Nineteen

THE AMERICAN BRASS

The success or demise of any of Ansonia's industries deeply affected the community. The larger the company, the larger the impact. In the course of its eighty-one years, American Brass became one of the largest; and its fortunes reflected the evolution of the brass industries of the Lower Naugatuck Valley.

Many sublimely motivated men had been caught up in the pioneering spirit of metal work. They focused their energies on ventures of original enterprises, that splintered into tangents of new inventions and techniques that multiplied or changed, in the search for perfection. At the end of the nineteenth century after innovative work in many factories, a need for a consolidation of the main advances in copper and brass manufacturing became apparent.

✱

The American Brass Company can trace its origins to Waterbury, Connecticut, where in 1812, Aaron Benedict founded a company to make metal buttons. The progress of that endeavor was underway when in

155

1830, Anson G. Phelps brought the trade materials that enabled the company to get a firm business foothold and secure industrial investors from England. Many small copper and brass manufacturers continued to develop on the rivers and streams north of Ansonia.

In Walcottsville (Torrington), Anson made his first manufacturing capital investment in an 1832 partnership with Aaron Benedict, Israel Coe, Israel Holmes and others, to roll brass and make kettles. Anson later withdrew from the partnership and established his own Ansonia Brass and Battery Company. The original partnership developed into the Coe Brass Manufacturing Company.

Near the end of the nineteenth century, the Coe Brass Manufacturing Company and the Waterbury Brass Company agreed to consolidate their interests. In December 1899 they were joined by the Ansonia Brass & Copper Company (owned by Phelps-Dodge), to form the American Brass Company, with headquarters in Ansonia. Waterbury manufacturers, Benedict & Burnham and Holmes, Booth and Haydens later joined them. Then in 1903, the Birmingham Brass Company in Derby dismantled and moved to join the others in Ansonia.

Charles F. Brooker, a knowledgeable and talented nephew of Coe, was named as the first president of the American Brass Company. He was well experienced in the Coe Company, and aspired to improve the method of processing brass for the new company. He traveled many times to England and Germany to study their methods and machinery.

Finally Brooker found and developed what he wanted. It was a machine that would process a hot billet of brass and, under the pressure of a hydraulic ram, force the brass through a steel die that would endure the pressure of fifty-tons per inch. He installed America's first brass-extrusion machine in the American Brass in Ansonia.

(The Brass Industry of the United States)

Charles F. Brooker

The company continued to purchase more mills. Its three main plants were in Torrington, Waterbury, and Ansonia. It added mills in Buffalo, New York; Detroit, Michigan; Kenosha, Wisconsin; and in Toronto, Canada. The acquisitions made Ansonia's American Brass Company, Ltd. the largest company in the world making and handling brass.

In 1922, the Anaconda Copper Mining Company of Montana purchased it for $45 million. Then, working as a branch of Anaconda, the Ansonia firm continued to operate under its own name, with its corporate organization intact.

*

In 1925, the Connecticut Chamber of Commerce reported that Connecticut manufacturers had grown from twenty-five in 1857 to 3,996. Sixty-four of those were the brass industry plants in the greater Naugatuck Valley. Those sixty-four produced one-third of the total output of copper and brass goods in the United States. Connecticut had truly proven to be "The Manufacturing State" and its copper and brass industry led all other states of America.

More brass and copper sheet, wire, tube, and rod was manufactured in Ansonia's American Brass Mill than any other Anaconda mill. Key to their success was its patented extrusion and hot press method which proved superior to the rolling process used by competitors.

In Ansonia, it was the sheer force of the power of dedicated working men that fashioned a remarkable manufacturing contribution to the civilization of mankind. Connecticut continued to maintain the manufacturing lead in America, and Ansonia and Waterbury were its most important centers of brass and copper manufacturing. Anaconda, continued to grow, acquiring mills across America. It ultimately became the largest copper, zinc and brass mining and manufacturing company in the world.

When Anaconda finally ceased its copper mining and production operations in 1993, it was a stunning blow to Ansonia and to all of the other communities that had participated in its success. All Anaconda copper mills and manufacturing facilities were closed, leaving thousands of workers, including highly skilled machinists, unemployed throughout the Lower Naugatuck Valley.

However, when the Ansonia mill was closed some past employees of the American Brass Company organized an independent company and named it the Ansonia Copper and Brass Company. It occupies some of the former American Brass Buildings on Liberty Street. Workers there extrude and draw copper alloyed material to semi-finished forms of rod, bar, wire, flat-wire and large diameter seamless tubes. The Company includes research, manufacturing, and testing in its business, and has a branch in Waterbury.

Much has changed since 1845 when Anson and Almon provided waterpower for manufacturing industries in Ansonia. Today's reliance on gas, oil and electricity has created harsh financial and environmental burdens.

In neighboring Seymour, the Seymour-New Haven Copper Company (founded in 1845), most recently owned by Olin Corporation of Missouri, closed in April 2007 due to environmental and financial issues. The Ansonia Copper and Brass Company has been forced into a partial closing of the higher energy-consuming portion of its business in Ansonia, while it works toward generating its own electricity inside the plant. Its Waterbury branch continues to operate as usual.

(Sharon L.C.M. Kelly)

Ansonia Copper and Brass
Company Office

Chapter Twenty

PHELPS DODGE CORPORATION

The founding of the manufacturing village of Ansonia was the crowning point of Anson's metal trade career. He had calculated that the instrumental move of adding a manufacturing division to diversify his newly organized Phelps–Dodge Company into industry would assure its continued success. The fact that the company is still making headlines is testimony to the overall success of his plan.

Anson's death marked the end of an era. His son-in-law, James B. Stokes, with two sons, left the firm two years later to concentrate on their Wall Street banking business. When Anson's partner, son-in-law, William Earl Dodge later retired, he remained as a consultant until he died in 1883. The next generations were left in control of the firm.

The Phelps-Dodge Company proudly continued to follow and reinforce the business principles established by its founders, and copper continued to be the key to its ongoing success. The metal's long history in the corporation continues to be a fascinating business saga, which includes the fact that the commodity quotation of copper has changed from thirty-five cents a pound in 1917 to three dollars and sixty-three cents in 2007.

When industrial expansions began to deplete the trade supply of copper in this country, Anson had imported it from Europe. But decades later, Phelps-Dodge realized that the sources of copper abroad were insufficient for the needs of American industries and began a search for mines in this country.

Fortuitously in 1881, William Church extended an invitation to have the company invest in a copper mine he discovered in Arizona. The mine proved to be in such an exceedingly rich copper area that Phelps-Dodge found itself in the enviable, but problematical position of having an excess of copper.

The responsibilities of tending to that first extremely rich mine, along with other rich mines, demanded company concentration. Due to the ramifications of mining and the intricacies of processing metal, Phelps-Dodge Company changed from an import-export business to one that specialized in the mining and handling of copper. In 1917, it legally became the Phelps-Dodge Corporation.

When an overabundance of copper became a problem for the Corporation, a 1935 solution was much the same as Anson had found when he had an overabundance of industrial metals in 1834. Phelps-Dodge turned to concentrate on developing its manufacturing division. The company added merchandising and service, and stellar success resulted.

✳

The average person does not fully appreciate how essential a component copper is for the innumerable conveniences and technological advances that impact our lives every day. We may first think of copper as part of such things as penny coins, telephones, appliances, computers, vehicles, cathodes, and plumbing equipment yet not know that it was Phelps-Dodge that provided the copper for the first transcontinental cables.

Other uses not often considered include the one-tenth inch thick, eighty-one and three-tenth ton, copper cladding utilized as the underwear for the Statue of Liberty; and the thirty-five to fifty pounds of copper used in a car. There are six hundred pounds of pipes and wiring in an average house. Typically post-industrial homes in America use twenty pounds of copper or more in electric motors, clocks, refrigerators, and computers. Five thousand kilowatts of electricity for a city requires a ton of copper. Other applications include those for the bottoms of ships, percussion caps for ammunition, large kettles, railways, and great miscellany of other uses.

✱

Other metals are also found in copper mines. Molybdenum, for one, is used for jet engine parts, pollution control devices, lubricants, space shuttle devices, high performance bicycles, and in the processes that alloy steel. Phelps-Dodge has molybdenum mines and processing facilities abroad in the United Kingdom and the Netherlands, as well as in Iowa and Colorado. In Texas and Arizona, Phelps-Dodge mines and refines not only copper and copper sulfate, but also silver, gold, and selenium.

The products engineered or manufactured by the corporation help bring energy to homes, businesses, telecommunications, and the special chemical sectors worldwide. In North America, Asia, Latin America, and Europe, Phelps-Dodge produces enamels, bare conductors, specialty wires, and high-performance conductors that link communities and contribute to the global economy. The corporation is also among the world's largest producers of carbon black that gives rubber its strength, makes tires last longer, fortifies plastics, and gives inks and toners their color. The twelve carbon black plants in nine countries make it the industry leader in pigmentation for coatings, inks and plastics.

Globally there are more than thirty Phelps Dodge (the name is no longer hyphenated) manufacturing facilities in seventeen countries that including Australia, Brazil, Canada, Chile, India, Indonesia, Mexico, and Peru.

*

In early 2001, Phelps Dodge made the transition at the Morenci Mine from the conventional mining, milling, smelting, and refining methods to the mine-for-leach process. Its total conversion process produced 99.99% pure copper accompanied with conservation of energy consumption, a ten-percent saving in the cost of production and product price, and produced no sulfur dioxide into the environment.

*

On May 21, 2005 at 4 p.m., the Phelps Dodge Corporation, which was divided into Mining and Manufacturing Divisions, rang the closing bell at the New York Stock Exchange. It was in commemoration of its seventy-fifth anniversary on the exchange. In 1929, there were 846 companies on the exchange; in 2005, there were 2780, only eighty-six of which were listed before 1929.

*

The Manufacturing Division of Phelps Dodge Corporation that was born in the Lower Naugatuck Valley of Connecticut developed into Phelps Dodge Industries, active in nineteen countries in the Americas, Africa and Asia. It continues to expand its global network of sales and manufacturing facilities, technological resources, and customized services. The company supplies markets worldwide with products for the power, construction, oil, gas, mining, telecommunication, and original equipment manufacturing businesses. Phelps Dodge prides itself on being just "One Company," a distinguished member within global communities of different languages, cultures, and traditions.

The Phelps Dodge Industries is comprised of three main manufacturing divisions:

(1) The Columbian Chemicals Company, which produces carbon black for inks, plastics, paints, electrical cable, and for the strength of tires, has facilities throughout the world and four manufacturing operations in North America (Arkansas, Kansas, Louisiana, and West Virginia).

(2) The Phelps Dodge Magnet Wire Company, with manufacturing facilities in Kentucky, Texas, North Carolina, and Mexico, is the world's largest producer of magnet wire, and of insulated conductors, used in electrical systems.

(3) The Phelps Dodge High Performance Conductors Headquarters in South Carolina produces tubing and specialty film-insulated conductors for the aerospace and electronic industries, at six locations, in Georgia, New Jersey and South Carolina.

Phelps Dodge Industries continues as the main supplier of such copper products as long rods, bare conductors, building wires, power cables, flexible cords, control cables, and industrial mining, communication, automotive cables, and the wire and cable products engineered principally for the global energy sector. The Company also provides aluminum bare conductors, building wire, power cable, secondary UD cable, service entry cable, and covered line cable.

✱

The long ago vision and work of Anson Greene Phelps to insure that his Phelps-Dodge Company

165

would be in position to participate in the industries of the future weathered through the centuries.

History, of course, is created every day and moves on. November 17, 2006, financial news reported that the Phelps Dodge Phoenix-based mining giant, employing 13,500 people worldwide, would be bought by Freeport-McMoRan Copper and Gold Corporation, which had won permission from the European Commission. The Mining Division of Phelps Dodge was comprised of large copper operations in the United States, Mexico, Chile, Peru, and Congo.

Freeport-McMoRan Copper and Gold, Inc. trades under the FCX symbol, and smelts and refines copper in Spain and Indonesia. In Indonesia, it mines copper, gold, and silver. Its Grasberg Mine is said to have the largest copper and gold reserves in the world.

A much smaller company than Phelps Dodge, Freeport-McMoRan paid eighteen billion dollars in cash and almost eight billion dollars in shares for the Phelps Dodge Mining Division. The acquisition made Freeport-McMoRan the world's largest publicly traded copper mining company.

The combined headquarters, of Freeport-McMoRan Copper & Gold Inc. and its subsidiary, Phelps Dodge Industries, is in Phoenix, Arizona. The Indonesian operations office for accounting and administrative functions remains in New Orleans.

Then on September 12, 2007, the Freeport-McMoRan Company, operating as Phelps Dodge International Corporation, sold its global wire and cable business to raise money for business. The buyer, General Cable Corporation of Kentucky, will profit by enhancing its leadership into countries worldwide.

❋

Thus, the dedicated work of eighteenth century orphan, Anson Greene Phelps, continues to burgeon.

PART V

SEEDS OF HOPE

E PLURIBUS UNUM

Chapter Twenty-One

ANSONIA HOUSES OF WORSHIP

Ansonia, within its comparatively small size of six and two-tenths square miles, was known for its record of having more churches than any other city in Connecticut. The many immigrants, who were attracted to Anson's village to work for a better life, naturally employed the new freedom to establish their own churches. It was also inevitable that whatever happened in Ansonia would affect the emerging nation.

Anson Phelps created his manufacturing village in the northern part of the area named Old Derby. A few English immigrants had settled there in 1654 on land where the Paugasett tribe of the Algonquin Nation was living.

In the beginning, the natives were very helpful to the immigrants. However, their basic belief that the land belonged to everyone, clashed sharply with that of the new settlers, who believed in "property rights." Bloody conflicts resulted. In the end, the number of English settlers and immigrants from the West Indian trade route began to increase and that of the natives diminished.

Old Derby, a community of Puritans, became a borough in 1675. The Puritans required the experience of a personal religious conversion to obtain church membership, which was required to receive Holy Communion, and to have the privilege of voting in civic affairs. Younger generations challenged these ideas and a large number in the community felt the church requirements were rigid and unacceptable. Coincidental with the timing of the First Religious Revival Period of 1735-1750, many members, led by John Holbrook and seven others, decided to change their type of church government. In 1737, they began holding services privately with missionaries; then, following the European precedent, they separated from their church. In 1747, the new membership constructed a House of Worship, called Christ's Church near the 1620 cemetery on Elm Street in Old Derby.

(Derby Historical Society)

Christ's Church
1747

One of the first things that the devout Anson Phelps did, upon designing his village, was to donate to the Congregational membership, a piece of land on the southern cliff of Ansonia, where he and his surveyor first stood viewing the valley.

At the beginning of 1848, part of the 1820 Congregationalist membership of the Old Derby parish left to join the Ansonia group at Colburn Street Hall. In 1852 the Ansonia Congregational Church was completed on the southern cliff.

In 1863, that wooden church was destroyed by fire. A replacement, constructed of Seymour fieldstone, was erected two years later at the same site of 34 South Cliff Street.

Anson donated a piece of land facing the Green on Elizabeth Street in Birmingham, for the construction of the Second Congregational Church, completed in 1846. He also presented an ample piece of his property on the corner of Elizabeth and Cottage streets in Birmingham to the Irish Catholic immigrants, who had worked in the Phelps-Smith copper mill, and were still without a place to worship, fifteen years later.

The grateful membership participated in digging a foundation for the structure. The first Saint Mary's Church was erected in time for an 1852 dedication.

The size of that church property allowed for major renovations and reconstruction of the building when membership increased. Thirty years later, an impressively large Saint Mary's Church, a rectory, a school, and a convent for the Sisters of Mercy were constructed.

(Derby Historical Society)

First Congregational Church
1852

(Derby Historical Society)

First Congregational Church
1865

(Derby Historical Society)
The Second Congregational Church
1846

(Derby Historical Society)
Saint Mary's Church
1852

(Derby Historical Society)

Saint Mary's Church
Rectory, Convent and School
1882

✳

The skilled industrialists who developed Ansonia made several trips to England and Germany (where the Industrial Era began in 1790), seeking manufacturing expertise. While there, they encouraged metal and textile workers to move to the promising new American manufacturing village. The workers were doubly attracted by the prospect of jobs and freedom to worship.

The English, Irish, Scottish, Scandinavian, and German were the first workers to come. Their goal was to build a better life in a new and better place.

Dedication to that common goal forged a strong bond within the diversity of their ethnic origins.

To improve their lives in the "New World" required working together. The achievement of their reigning lifestyle produced the long-lived American credo that led to success. To those proud settlers and their progeny, just being born in, or migrating to America did not make an "American." Only adopting the practice of the country's philosophy of working together toward a better tomorrow could accomplish that.

Each successive nationality that arrived in the Ansonia village of Connecticut's original English settlers created a network of social and financial support. Such organizations as "The Prins Gustav Lodge," the "Bee Hive," and "The Svedish Vasa Order of America" supported the Swedish people. "The Lady MacDonald" and "The Clan MacDonald Lodges" were the Scottish societies. The Germans had their "Order of the Sons of Herman and Brunhildea."

Later, the Ukrainians organized the "St. Peter and Paul Mutual Benefit Association" and the Russians supported "The Brotherhood of St. Basil the Great." The Polish relied on "The Falcons," and the Lithuanians on "The St. Anthony Society."

Each group planned to build a suitable place for their families to focus on the lessons for living taught in the Bible, and in which to praise the Lord in gratitude. Their support organizations made it possible to accumulate sufficient funds to get permission from the church bureaucracies and to establish the churches they needed for spiritual strength and personal solace. Groups met at private homes or halls while waiting for their churches to be constructed.

The variety of church architecture became notable. Divisions within the mother churches occurred, as the congregations grew. After distinctions were drawn, they divided and separated into other congregations.

The Methodist Episcopalians separated from what had been the 1793 Christ's Church. They began by worshipping in a schoolhouse; and in 1837, constructed the first church to be built on the Birmingham Green.

In 1848, some members of that Birmingham church moved to Ansonia and attended the first official meeting of the Methodist Episcopal Society of Ansonia. Membership meetings were held in the private home of James Booth until 1851, then the society established its Hall of Worship above a few stores at the corner of Main and Bartlett (Bridge) streets. Their church was completed and dedicated on April 22, 1865. It was located on Main Street, across from the Maple Street Bridge and the *Naugatuck Valley Sentinel* building.

✳

In 1849 the Episcopalians of Christ's Church of Old Derby merged with the St. James Church of Birmingham, and in 1851, established the Trinity Church at the corner of Main and Tremont streets in Ansonia.

Property for a new Christ Church at 56 South Cliff Street was purchased and donated by Franklin Farrel in 1893. Located across the street from the Ansonia Library, it was next to the Cliff Walk and the Congregational Church. The church on Main Street was vacated in 1900.

The tower of that Christ Church and the tall spire of the Congregational Church provide a distinguishing skyline, seen above the trees on the southeastern cliff.

(Scrap Book)

First Methodist Episcopal Church,
Main Street
1865
(Horse Railway and Newspaper Office)

(150th Anniversary Booklet)
Trinity Church-
Christ Episcopal Church
Main Street Corner of Tremont Street
1851

(Sharon L.C.M. Kelly)

Tower of Christ Episcopal Church

(Sharon L.C.M. Kelly)

Skyline of East Ansonia

(Derby Historical Society)

Christ Episcopal Church
1900

✺

The Irish, who had worked in the manufacturing area of Birmingham, were attracted to the village of Ansonia. In 1853, they started a Roman Catholic Sunday School there. Then, in 1868, those members constructed a Roman Catholic Church of the Assumption of the Blessed Virgin Mary, on the corner of Main and Cheever streets in Ansonia, and left the Birmingham Saint Mary's Church.

(Derby Historical Society)

First Roman Catholic Church
of The Assumption
1868

In 1889, Phelps Dodge Company sold its property on North Cliff Street for them to build a larger church to accommodate their ever-increasing Irish Catholic membership. After eighteen years of construction work, the new church was completed. Its monumental, imposing edifice can be seen from across the Naugatuck River.

(Derby Historical Society)
Roman Catholic Church Of The Assumption
1907

*

Congregations that represented the later arriving immigrants from other countries also became busy building churches. The Swedish Methodist Episcopalians began meeting at private homes in 1889, and in 1903 completed their church construction at the corner of Arch and Franklin streets. Originally those immigrants held services in the Swedish language, but by 1934 English had become their language of choice,

and they changed the name of the church to Trinity
Methodist Episcopal Church.

(One-Hundredth Anniversary Booklet)
Swedish Methodist Church
1903

When fire destroyed the First Methodist Episcopal
Church on Main Street on December 14, 1943,

185

the Swedish congregation invited the members to worship with them at their church on Arch Street. As

(Anniversary Booklet)
Ansonia First Methodist Episcopal Church
Main Street

a result, a greater plan of merging developed, and with a combination of resources, property at the corner of Holbrook Place and Franklin Street was purchased.

Ground was broken on June 11, 1950, and in 1951, a church with an in-resident rectory was constructed and dedicated as The United Methodist Church. The bell, hanging in the spire that was crafted by Farrel-Birmingham, had been salvaged from the original church. It was presented in 1866 by The Honorable Charles H. Pine, in memory of his grandmother, Mrs. Wooster.

(Sharon L.C.M. Kelly)
United Methodist Church Spire
Crafted by Farrel Company

(One Hundredth Anniversary Booklet)
United Methodist Church
Franklin Street
1951

The church was built using ashlar type blocks of quarried Ohio sandstone. It faces southeast on Franklin Street hill, and presents a warm inviting Gothic style interior. A large arched stained glass window cased in pre-cast stone in the chancel is its focal point. The archway to the sanctuary conforms to the shape of the window. Among other windows on either side of the pews, there are stained glass memorials depicting, "The Home of Mary, Martha, and Lazarus," "The Ascension," and "Christ in Gethsemane."

Another Swedish group organized as the Swedish Lutheran Saint Paul Augustana Church in 1891. It too began meetings in a private home. Six years later the members purchased what had been the original Christ Church building on Main and Tremont streets.

Then, in 1913, the Swedish Lutherans moved

from Main Street to the stucco church that faces the Howard Avenue intersection at 35 Jackson Street. Members later divided into two groups. One joined the Trinity Lutheran Church in Shelton; the other joined the Immanuel Lutheran Church in Seymour. The building was left vacant until 1944, when the Saint Peter and Saint Paul Catholic War Veterans Post 1677, Inc. purchased the building. Later it was sold to the Evangel Temple Church of God in Christ, Inc.

(Sharon L.C.M. Kelly)
Swedish Lutheran Church

The First Baptist Church in Ansonia was constructed at the head of Main Street on State Street's Foundry Hill in 1881.

(Derby Historical Society)
First Baptist Church (note arc light))

It excelled as a host for other groups of members waiting to build their churches. In its first year, it fostered the First Baptist Church of Shelton, then, it welcomed an African-American congregation for worship until its Macedonia Baptist Church was constructed on Clifton Avenue (Pershing Drive) in Ansonia.

(Derby Historical Society)

Macedonia Baptist Church
1893

The landmark First Baptist Church on State Street Foundry Hill continued its work; it welcomed the Italian Baptist membership that was waiting to establish its Italian Mission of Ansonia.

Many decades later, several circumstances including a lack of parking, in the downtown vicinity, led the church membership to build a new church on Prindle Avenue. The new more modern building graces the hilltop area of the city on a spacious piece of property.

(Derby Historical Society)

First Baptist Church
Prindle Avenue

Since that time the historic First Baptist Church landmark building has remained at the head of Main Street. The structure's original function and grandeur have been lost, yet it may be a reassuring sight for some.

✻

In 1909, the Catholic Italians bought what had been the original Roman Catholic Church of the Assumption at the corner of 451 Main and Cheever streets. The wooden building, surrounded by stores and tenement housing for factory workers, was renamed, the Holy Rosary Roman Catholic Church.

In 1955, when the Connie and Diane Hurricanes struck, the ensuing flood destroyed lower Main Street and the church. A new Holy Rosary Church was erected in a reconstructed area of Ansonia's Lower Main Street, on a new road named Father Salemi Drive. The congregation chose a beautiful round design, in white stone, showcasing multiple stained glass windows. The structure suggests a regal crown reigning over its beautifully landscaped foreground.

(Derby Historical Society)
Holy Rosary Roman Catholic Church

*

Russian Immigrants from Austro-Hungarian Galicia (present day Slovakia) petitioned the bishop of Alaska and the Aleutian Islands, in 1895, to accept their Brotherhood of St. Basil the Great Membership as a congregation of the Russian Orthodox Church. They purchased property at the eastern corner of Howard

Avenue and Crescent Street in 1899, and constructed their church the following year.

In 1954, fire destroyed the church. Its sister church, on Hubbell Avenue, the Holy Trinity Greek Orthodox Church, invited the congregation to share its church and conduct separate services, while their new church was being built.

The original church bells that had been donated by Czar Nicholas II and Czarina Alexandra of Russia were saved and placed in the new church in 1956. The image medallions with dedicating inscriptions and *The Transfiguration of Christ* on the south transept, inside the new Three Saints Church, merit special notice.

(Derby Historical Society)
Sanctuary Gates
Three Saints Russian Orthodox Church

The church's 15th Century Classic Novgorodian style of art and iconography has attracted many visitors to 26 Howard Avenue. Russian artist, Pimen Sofronof, frescoed a totally unique masterpiece inside the church. The church is regarded as one of the most beautiful in the eastern United States.

Pimen Sofronof also painted icons for the Syrian church in Bergenfield, New Jersey, and has decorated the interiors of Russian Churches in Brooklyn and Syracuse, New York.

(Sharon L.C.M. Kelly)
Icons above Main Entrance

(Sharon L.C.M. Kelly)
Three Saints Russian Orthodox Church
Main Entrance

(Derby Historical Society)
Three Saints Russian Orthodox Church
1956

The golden 120-foot central spire of the Three Saints Church creates an identifying skyline, when viewed from the East Side of the Naugatuck River. It is coupled in silhouette with one of the most prominent green oxidized copper domes, crowning the neighboring Saint Peter and Saint Paul Ukrainian Greek Catholic Church.

(Sharon L.C.M. Kelly)
Western Skyline

197

*

The beautiful Saint Peter and Saint Paul domed church was the fulfillment of the dreams and work of the first immigrants from the Austro-Hungarian Empire, (now Ukraine, Poland, Czech Republic, Slovak Republic, Hungary, and Romania). They began to settle in areas near Ansonia in 1884, and represented the faith of the Ukrainian Catholics as well as the Slovak Catholics of the Byzantine (Greek) Rite. Joining together for mutual practical support and spiritual ministry, they worked to establish one of the first parishes of the Ukrainian Greek Catholic Church in the United States.

The cornerstone of the first church was laid in 1897 on 9 May Street at the corner of Bassett Street.

(Centennial Yearbook)

Russian Greek Catholic Church
Of Saint Peter and Saint Paul
1898

(Centennial Yearbook)

Saint Peter and Saint Paul
Ukrainian Greek Catholic Church
1915

In 1910 the membership purchased property for a larger church on Clifton Avenue from the Colonel Wooster family. The daunting intricacies of creating the spectacular church were overcome by the complete dedication of its parishioners. They went so far as to offer their homes as collateral for the project.

The yellow brick church is a landmark, and visible from the neighboring town of Derby. Its huge five domes projecting above the red tile roof are covered with copper that has turned a patinated green.
Inside, the church walls are covered with Numidian-style marble. The main altar was originally of white marble, but so slippery it was replaced.

Elizabeth Crossland Matricaria

(Centennial Yearbook)
Aerial View
Saint Peter and Saint Paul
Ukrainian Greek Greek Catholic Church

200

In 1916, the noted artist Theodore Hladky, from Galicia, decorated the inside of the domes in Byzantine style. Stained glass windows complement the main dome.

Inside the church, there are murals, and stained glass windows, as well as statues. An iconostas, with doors and tiers of icons, separates the altar from the nave.

(Courtesy of Reverend Pawlo Martyniuk)
Iconostas

Unlike the original church that had pews on the sides for the elderly, and standing space in the center of the church for others, this church offers a multitude of long oak pews facing the altar for all worshippers.

(Courtesy of Reverend Pawlo Martyniuk)
Main Church Area

In 1965, the Saint Peter and Saint Paul neighboring Parochial School on Howard Avenue opened. The school excelled in its reputation and parents eagerly sought enrollment for their young children. However, in 1994, the building was sold to be used as a Head Start School for disadvantaged children.

In 1981, the name of the city street, at the side of the church connecting Howard and Clifton avenues, was officially changed from Short Street to Father Lar Drive, to honor the work accomplished by Reverend Basil Lar.

(Centennial Year Book)
Saint Peter and Saint Paul School
1965

*

The Holy Trinity Greek Orthodox immigrants also brought their work ethic and deep faith in God to Ansonia. At first, they had to travel to Bridgeport to attend church; then, in 1915, they began renting the Ukrainian Church Hall on May Street. Their numbers increased and, in 1917, a building fund was started.

Six young men of the congregation dug the foundation for a church at Two Hubbell Avenue, and the Ansonia Savings Bank signed a note to complete the building in 1919. Donations from its congregation and other well wishers made possible the completion of the inside of the church. One of the donors was Mrs. Alton Farrel, who gave the choir loft. The belfry bell was purchased from the St. Peter and St. Paul Ukrainian Church.

The first church service of The Holy Trinity Greek Orthodox Church was held on Easter in 1920. At the dawn of that day, a tradition of roasting lambs on an outdoor spit for a community Easter dinner began. The last roast at the church took place in 1976, since then the tradition continues at family homes.

*

Russian and Ukrainian immigrants who followed a Russian missionary established the Evangelical Baptist membership in 1919. As a separate entity, they too worshipped at the First Baptist Church. After the merger of the Methodists, they purchased the original Swedish Methodist building, at the corner of Arch and Franklin streets in 1950.

*

In 1894, Connecticut's first German Congregational Church was built at the corner of Beaver and Tremont streets. By 1911, its membership conducted Sunday School services in the English language. The name of the church was changed by the membership to Pilgrim Congregational Church in 1941; then, in 1964, the church united with the First Congregational Church of Ansonia on South Cliff Street. A Dutch congregation hosted by the German church, also joined the First Congregational Church.

(Sharon L.C.M. Kelly)

Holy Trinity Greek Orthodox Church
1920

205

(Derby Historical Society)

German Congregational Church
1894

❋

The Lithuanians settled in Ansonia, and convened in 1912 to make plans for their church. They completed the construction of the Saint Anthony of Padua Lithuanian Roman Catholic Church at 199 North Main Street in 1915. The membership contributed much to the citizenship of Ansonia. In 1935, they sponsored the Lithuanian Political Club to study American government, and organized the Sviesos Draugija Society to concentrate on education.

(Derby Historical Society)

Saint Anthony of Padua
Lithuanian Roman Catholic Church
1915

❋

The Polish Catholics worshipped at St. Michael's Church in Derby for almost two decades before leaving in 1924 with 280 members for Ansonia. Their first mass was held in a rented hall on Colburn (Central) Street. A year later, they laid the cornerstone at 32 Jewett Street for the St. Joseph Church, convent, chapel, and school. Upon completion the parishioners beautified the church grounds.

(Sharon L.C.M. Kelly)

Saint Joseph's Church

Father Janowski served the church for twenty-five years. His heartfelt wish was to have a place in a country setting where his parishioners could enjoy outings and picnics; and in 1933, he planned the purchase of 34.6 acres of forested land, about two miles north from the church on the Pulaski Highway. It belonged to the Ansonia Water Company and featured a pond and a small brook running through a portion of the land. The price was $2,750.

As a gift to the church and to commemorate the twenty-fifth jubilee of Father Janowski, the St. Stanislaus Parish of New Haven joined in donating the property to the church. The park was named Warzawa in honor of the capital city of the homeland of many parishioners.

Building began in 1934, and continued to include a pavilion, cabins, a hall, camping area, swings, seesaws, and a grand ballroom. The place was popularly known as Warsaw Park. It became the site of many social events, not only for the Polish community, but also for public events.

✱

In 1893, Jewish immigrants requested a charter from the secretary of state to build a place of worship in Ansonia. When granted, they constructed the Beth-El Synagogue on Colburn (Central) Street.

(Sharon L.C.M. Kelly)
Original Beth El Synagogue

There were two factions within the group and a conflict over procedures and prayers led the Sephardim to break away from the Ashkanazes in 1916 and build another synagogue, B'nai Jacob, on Factory Street (Chestnut Street). However, in keeping with the original charter, the name of the building was changed to Beth-El.

In 1933, after the factions remedied their disagreements, the two Jewish congregations merged into one, and conducted services at the Factory Street Beth-El Synagogue.

(Derby Historical Society)

Beth-El Synagogue
1916

❋

The African-Americans had organized as the Zion Mission in 1874 and occupied a building on the corner of New Haven Avenue and Gilbert Street. They moved to Birmingham in 1881 and in 1888 erected a church building on Derby Avenue.

In 1931, they moved to the Luria Block on Main Street, Ansonia. When the B'Nai Jacob membership of the 96 Colburn Street original Beth-El Synagogue vacated the building in 1933, the African-American group relocated there and named the building the Zion American Methodist Episcopal Church.

✱

Another African-American group named the Church of God in Christ organized in 1929. In 1959, it purchased the remaining synagoguc, the Beth-El building on Factory (Chestnut) Street, after its Jewish membership left Ansonia.

Cleveland Williams had been the pastor of that African-American congregation in 1938. He became a bishop in 1944 and was given jurisdiction over three New England states. Later he was made the international superintendent of their church schools and the president of their international convention. The Church Of God in Christ membership, which Williams had served as an elder, now proudly bears his name on a memorial plaque and service message in front of their church building.

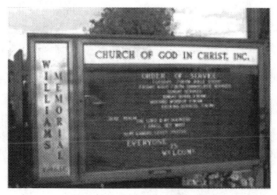

Sharon L.C.M.Kelly)
Church Bulletin

The street where it is located was formerly called Factory Street, then later, Chestnut Street; now the area of the church is named Williams Street, and the address of the church is 95 Bishop Williams Court.

*

In 1930 an invitation was sent to African-Americans in Ansonia by Father Edwards of St. Luke's Episcopal Church in New Haven to attend his services. The group founded the St. John's Mission in Ansonia on South Main Street not far from Division Street. Services were held there until the Mission merged with the St. James Episcopal Church in Derby in 1964.

*

A Salvation Army Building is now on Lester Street, at the corner of High Street. The present Ansonia building was constructed after the 1955 flood destroyed its storefront building on Main Street.

(Sharon L.C.M. Kelly)

Main Entrance
Salvation Army Building

The Salvation Army was organized in London in 1865. Evangelical members of the Salvation Army extend worldwide, offering practical adaptations of the Word of God to light the way of humanity. It is a hard-working, down-to-earth membership, and one tends to forget it is a volunteer religious organization whose membership is dependent upon donations to accomplish its Good Works.

Many stories from war veterans and disaster victims about the corps' unexcelled assistance bear testimony to their life-preserving role. Daily, the Salvation Army helps in the rehabilitation of the morally, spiritually, and physically needy. In Ansonia it also offers summer programs for youngsters.

✱

The Star of Bethlehem, an Apostolic Church is also located on Lester Street.

(Sharon L.C.M. Kelly)

Star of Bethlehem Church
1953

✱

In 1887, the Immanuel Episcopal Church was erected on the corner of Church Street and Howard Avenue. In 1928, it was replaced by the present stone structure at 6 Church Street.

The congregation later merged with the St. James Church in Derby. Then in 1996, the structure became the Anglican Church of the Resurrection.

(Sharon L.C.M. Kelly)

The Anglican Church of the Resurrection
1996

✱

Newer church groups and storefront churches can be found in the City of Ansonia. One of the storefront churches is located at 244 Main Street across from City Hall. It is named the Iglesia Cristiana La Rosa de Saron.

(Sharon L.C.M. Kelly)

Inglesia Cristiana La Rosa de Saron

*

America grew to twenty million immigrants between 1870 and 1910. They brought their faith with them and built churches across the nation.

The population was so overwhelming that a series of immigration restriction laws were passed in 1920. Time was needed to adjust the infrastructure of the country to accommodate the growing number of immigrants.

Although time has changed many things, Ansonians still have the opportunity to find cultural stability and a common grounding of faith in their churches. The memberships are not as clearly defined by ethnicity as they once were, and attendance is not as universal. Housings may be more or less formal; yet the sturdy original church buildings can still be found.

The congregations usually occupy their original churches, yet groups within the memberships shift and still spawn new churches. In some instances, groups adopt vacated churches and rename them. In others, memberships diminish and church finances become a problem. If indicated by circumstances, churches share leaders or buildings. Some of the population is cynical, yet many continue to search for an ideal group in which to sustain faith and hope.

*

The manufacturing village of Ansonia was a microcosm of the cultural face of America. It exercised its religious freedoms and work ethic in a potpourri of ethnicity.

Dedicated and united, American immigrants strove for, and practiced beneficence and civilized deportment. The momentous result of the free blending of religious faiths and nationalities produced a nation so unique, the country became tenaciously ready, able, and willing to extend hope to the world.

EPILOGUE

Anson Greene Phelps was heir to the period of mercantile trade. His was a time of sublime motivations, struggles to survive, succeed, and to share. Men were intent upon learning from their heritage of human endeavors.

As an eminent trader of metals, he began to participate in industrial capitalism. Although capitalism was known in the world under other regimes, it was necessarily unique in the hands of the multinational settlers living in the new free America.

Anson was an eminently devout man and conducted his business with an unwavering dedication to ethical values. At one with the times, he became a talented leader in trade and philanthropy. When he founded Ansonia, his vision was, not only to give balance to his Phelps-Dodge Company, but also to benefit his fellowman and strike a blow against poverty.

As decades passed, American capitalism continued to expand, prosperity dipped, and then rose higher within the freedoms of the united nation. Against tyranny, under the rule of law, and with respect for individuals, America's system of government proved to have the greatest power and fewest drawbacks. The span of human life lengthened, poverty lessened, and wondrous possibilities for all humankind blossomed.

Principled men continued the work of setting templates to help in the search for a civilized, fair world. Necessarily that promise of a fair world was left for succeeding generations to safeguard and advance.

Elizabeth Crossland Matricaria
Avon, Connecticut
March 2013

THE FAIR WORLD

Far beyond the many mountains, steep and stony
without wear, Past the crimson man-made fountains,
bones of children bleached and bare,
Far beyond--but it is there!

There the fair world blooming glistens, Hate and Death
there never roam,
And the wayfarer who listens hears the language spoken
home;
There no Babylon confusions from man's clashing speeches
sprung,
Only throats' attuned effusions in a universal tongue.

In the forum of that region all possess the rank of kings;
Yellow coolies by the legion drawing water at the springs
Ebony and copper races fraternizing there as one
With maroon and milky faces mingling smiling in the sun;

Equal privilege for pleasure. Every dwelling is an inn,
Where the warmth of heart is measure, not the tinting of
the skin.
Mankind there sequesters Sorrow, clasps the first
primeval bond,
In the fair world of Tomorrow *far beyond and far
beyond.*

Like a murdered pixie risen from a bivouac of biers,
Love repudiates her prison, bursting national frontiers.
Brotherhood prevails. The sages ponder on the past, and
then
How the babes may with the ages grow more nearly perfect
men.

Warriors plan grand successes, not with tickets to the
tomb,
But to vanquish wildernesses and make rhododendrons
bloom.
Hail, O men, the faultless wonder! Justice reckons _open-
eyed_,
They have torn her mask asunder and iniquity has died!

Shadows and low tuneful noises, now when day and night
have kiss'd,
Bring to view the varied poises where men worship as they
list.
Have ye spied the sweating peasant pause in rapture in the
mead,
Or the soldier without malice pensive in sepulchral lines?
These have glimpsed a kingdom pleasant with a
philanthropic creed,
Glimpsed the dream of dreams a-waiting in a cottage by
cool pines;

They have seen the hallowed fountains of the fair world
drown Despair,
Far beyond the many mountains where no mortal seems
to dare.
Far beyond--but it is there!

Dorio Anthony Matricaria
1937

(1941)

ACKNOWLEDGMENTS

I appreciate the encouragement of friends and professionals who supported me in my effort to bring Anson and Ansonia into the limelight with this first of my two books. I acknowledge the following people for:

Editing suggestions

Rita Robinson, Cincinnati, OH
Sharon L.C.M. Kelly, Avon, CT
Lynn Zelem, Derby CT
John Walter, Martha's Vineyard, MA

Sandra Malard, Devon, PA

Material verifications

S.E. Simon, Simsbury Historical Society, Simsbury, CT
Robert Novack, Jr., Derby Historical Society, Derby, CT

Sandra Markham, New York Historical Society, New York, NY

Alice Pentz, Research Librarian, Avon Library, Avon, CT

Cecilia Roberts, Research Librarian, Simsbury Library, Simsbury, CT

Mary Ann Capone, Assistant Library Director, Ansonia, CT

Charles Seccombe, Historian, City of Ansonia, CT

George Curtis, Historian, Eagle Hose, Hook and Ladder Company, Ansonia, CT

Franklin Farrel III, Secretary (retired) Farrel Company, North Branford, CT

James L. Burns, Vice President, Farrel Corporation, Ansonia, CT

Barbara Gona Tchakiridis, Historian, United Methodist Church, Ansonia. CT

Lois A. Young, Historian, Christ Church, Ansonia, CT

Michael T. W. Smerznak, Centennial Chairman, St. Peter and St. Paul Ukrainian Church, Ansonia, CT

Reverend Russell Waldmann, First United Methodist Church, Ansonia, CT

Father George Brower, St. James Church, Derby, CT

Father Kevin Donovan, St. Mary's Church, Derby, CT

Father Mark Sobezak, St. Joseph's Church, Ansonia, CT

Reverend James H. Smith, Holy Rosary Church, Ansonia, CT

Reverend Rocco Florenza, Anglican Church of the Resurrection, Ansonia, CT

Father Joel McEachen, Holy Trinity Greek Church, Ansonia, CT

Personal help

Sharon L.C.M. Kelly, Avon, CT

Halina Grata, Unionville, CT

BIBLIOGRAPHY

BOOKS

Carter, Paul Emory, editor *"The World's Fair Anthology of Verse"*
    The Exposition Press, New York 1938

Cleland, Robert Glass. *"A History of Phelps Dodge, 1834-1950"*
    Alfred A. Knopf, New York, 1952

Connecticut Chamber of Commerce, Inc. *"Facts about Connecticut"*
    1929 Finlay Brothers Press. Inc., Hartford, CT

Covington, Edward J. *"Franklin Silas Terry (1862-1926), Industrialist
    Paragon of Organization, Harmony and Generosity"* 1994

Derby Historical Society *"Images of America-Ansonia"*
    Arcadia Publishing, Charleston, SC, 1999

Derby Historical Society. *"Images of America-Derby"*
    Arcadia Publishing, Charleston, SC, 1999

Derby Historical Society. *"Then and Now-Derby and Ansonia 2004"*

Dodge, Phyllis B. *"Tales of the Phelps-Dodge Family-A Chronicle of
    Five Generations"* New York Historical Society

Durant, Will "Story of Civilization" Volume IV Simon and Shuster,
    NY 1950

Kuhns, Maude Pinney. *"The Mary and John"* Charles E. Tuttle
    Company, Rutland, VT and Tokyo, Japan 1943

Larson, Dorothy A. *"A History of Ansonia--Bicentennial 1976"*
    The Ansonia Bicentennial Commission
    William J. Mack Company, North Haven, CT 1976

Lathrop, William G. Mount of Carmel, CT. *"The Brass Industry in*
  "The United States" Wilson H. Lee Company, New Haven, CT 1926

Molloy, Leo T, editor. *"Tercentenary Pictorial and History of the*
  Lower Naugatuck Valley" Emerson Press, Inc., Ansonia, CT 1935

Novack, Michael. *"The Spirit of Democratic Capitalism"*
  Simon and Schuster, New York 1982

Osborne, Norris Galpin, editor. *"History of Connecticut" Volume IV*
  The State History Company, New York 1925

Phelps, Oliver Seymour of Portland, OR, Servin, Andrew of Lenox,
  MA *"The Phelps Family of America – Their English*
  Ancestors" Vol. II Eagle Publishing Company, Pittsfield,
  MA 1899

Rosenblum, Jonathan. *"The Copper Crucible"* ILR Press School of
  Industrial & Labor Relations,
  Cornell University, Ithaca, New York. 1995

Studley, G. L. *"Connecticut The Industrial Incubator"* The American
  Society of Mechanical Engineers. Hartford, CT 1981

Smerznak, Michael, editor *"St. Peter & St. Paul Centennial*
  Yearbook " Olan Mills, 1997

MICROFILM

Phelps, Anson Greene. *"The Anson Greene Phelps Papers"*
  "Diaries 1805-1853" Yale University Library Microfilm

BOOKLETS

The City of Ansonia. *"Commemorative Booklet 100th Anniversary*
  of the Founding of Ansonia" 1944

First Methodist Episcopal Church, Ansonia, CT
  "Dedication and 100th Anniversary"

First United Methodist Church, Ansonia, CT
  "The Flame Burns Brightly"

St. Joseph's Church, Ansonia, CT
  "*St. Joseph's 75th Anniversary Booklet*"

Christ Church, Ansonia, CT "*Christ Church 150th Commemorative Booklet*"

St. Peter and St. Paul Church, Ansonia, CT "*St. Peter and St. Paul Centennial Yearbook*"

NEWSPAPERS

The Ansonia Evening Sentinel
The New Haven Register
The Valley Drummer
The Valley Gazette
The Hartford Courant